Terms and Conc

LEGAL NOTICE

The Publisher has strived to be as accurate and complete as possible in the creation of this report, notwithstanding the fact that he does not warrant or represent at any time that the contents within are accurate due to the rapidly changing nature of the Internet.

While all attempts have been made to verify information provided in this publication, the Publisher assumes no responsibility for errors, omissions, or contrary interpretation of the subject matter herein. Any perceived slights of specific persons, peoples, or organizations are unintentional.

In practical advice books, like anything else in life, there are no guarantees of income made. Readers are cautioned to reply on their own judgment about their individual circumstances to act accordingly.

This book is not intended for use as a source of legal, business, accounting or financial advice. All readers are advised to seek services of competent professionals in legal, business, accounting and finance fields.

Table Of Contents

Foreword

Have you heard of the term: "Copywriting"? Wikipedia defined it as:

"Copywriting is the use of words and ideas to promote a person, business, opinion or idea. Although the word copy may be applied to any content intended for printing (as in the body of a newspaper article or book), the term copywriter is generally limited to promotional situations, regardless of the medium (as in advertisements for print, television, radio or other media).

The purpose of marketing copy, or promotional text, is to persuade the reader, listener or viewer to act—for example, to buy a product or subscribe to a certain viewpoint".

In the online marketing world, copywriting is used extensively to promote blog readership, get opt-ins for list building and to monetize your prospects using sales letters or video sales letters.

If you truly wish to be successful in your online business, you'll have to learn the ropes of effective copywriting so that your readers love you, your ads convert and you make $$$$.

Thankfully, good copywriting is a *learnable* skill.

The Copywriting Playbook

How To Make People Buy Your Sh*t,
Even If You Suck At Selling

Dedicated to all the teachers who called me a loser when I got kicked out of my *first* highschool – here's lookin' at you, kid ;)

Chapter 1:

Introduction

Synopsis

One of the most powerful skills you could have is the skill of writing words that make people want to give you money.

There's literally nothing else like it.

Imagine being in a financial pickle and needing some fast-cash to make rent, pay for hospital bills or simply travel the world.

With the power of good copy, you can literally write yourself a blank check, partner with the most elite marketers in the world and sell *almost* anything you can think of.

You can do this using nothing more than mere words.

Intro

Copywriting saved my life.

When I was 12 years old, I started in a martial art called Jeet Kune Do.

It was my first real introduction to self-improvement as a human being.

After more than 8 years of training, I was finally asked to help teach classes and sign people up.

This is when my instructor, Dwight Woods stressed the importance of understanding sales, human behavior and more importantly... *copywriting.*

You see, as he put it, if you can write copy and sell with "paper and ink" – you can sell <u>face to face.</u>

The principles are very much the same.

The thing is, when you learn how to build likeability and trust in your copy, you're able to transfer those same skills into "real life" encounters.

Having this almost magical ability to persuade and influence others gives you *hypnotist-like* abilities.

After going down the martial arts path and owning a couple schools with a business partner, I started becoming *really* interested in flipping websites.

See, I had people from Upwork.com who would make a website for around $500...

... and I was flipping them for $1500+.

How did I get customers?

It wasn't social media.

It was old school cold calling and banging on doors.

This point in my life taught me 2 things:

1. How to deal with rejection

And...

2. How to stay consistent

See, when you experience a lot of rejection, you build some thick skin and start understand what turns people on versus what turns them off.

I realized that after 150 cold calls, I would make 4 to 6 appointments.

Out of those 4 to 6 appointments I would close 1 or 2 people on a website.

This worked like *clockwork.*

The thing is, most folks wouldn't go through the 150 calls like my friends and I did when we were "slangin' sites."

So when people told us, "cold calls don't work" – we laughed in their face, called them a more derogatory term for "sissy" and kept on chugging along.

Little did we know, there *was* an easier way.

After building a relatively successful web design business, I tested out sending a direct mail letter.

And guess what?

My first letter for this little business of ours pulled in a 6% conversion!

If you don't know, the average in direct mail is 1-2%... so I was STOKED!

I quickly realized that this letter I wrote and mailed, got me the same results as 150 cold calls, except I didn't make the call... the prospects would CALL me to book an appointment. I couldn't believe how *simple* this all was.

Since then, I've been hooked and have sold products, *anonymously* in the following niches using nothing more than a 1 page website, a digital product and words...

- ✓ Software
- ✓ Dog Training
- ✓ Martial Arts
- ✓ Survival
- ✓ Self Development
- ✓ And a few more I'm forgetting to mention

Back in the day, the best copywriters were the great businesspersons of the olden days who knew how to sell anything to anybody. While people possessed powerful weapons, their most powerful weapon was their pen, typewriter or tongue (for face to face/phone sales).

Today, modern entrepreneurs are making a killing using copywriting techniques in their businesses. Keep in mind, selling things online can be harder than selling things offline because you lack the sincerity of voice and body language.

However, if you discover how to tap into the power of copywriting to illicit the emotions of your customers, you'll be laughing your way to the bank.

In the next few chapters, I'm going to reveal to you these secrets and do my very best to arm you with the *right* knowledge to take massive action and achieve great levels of success in your business.

Chapter 2:

Basics of Copywriting

Synopsis

Copywriting is used in many places throughout your online business funnel. In this section you will see common examples of where it is used.

The Basics

- ✓ Website content
- ✓ Blog posts
- ✓ Landing Pages
- ✓ Email Marketing
- ✓ Sales Pages
- ✓ Video Sales Letters

Remember, the ultimate goal of copywriting is to get your readers to perform your most desired outcome.

For example, making a purchase or signing up into your mailing list.

That's why it's very important that you clarify what your desired result is before you embark on your copywriting crusade.

Clarity is power.

It's important to know what you're after so that when you write, things will go the direction you want them to go.

Okay, let's look at some basics.

Keeping in mind that we want our readers to perform our most desired result, we also can't be too forceful.

Here's rule number one:

Keep it casual

You want to be seen as a friendly person who is also an authority figure in your field.

The last thing you want to appear like is a blatant salesman.

The latter will cause people to dislike you and even you as spam.

The next thing you must know is that some rules may not make sense at first.

But one thing that does make sense is this, these lessons have been tested (split-tested) and proven by top online marketers for years, so rather than trying to re-invent the wheel, follow what works and reap the rewards!

Sound fair?

Now, I strongly encourage you do some split testing of your own also.

Eliminate things that don't work and duplicate or multiply things that do – this the obvious advice MOST folks forget to do.

Next up, we'll look into one of the most important components of good copy – **headlines.**

Chapter 3:

Headline Essentials

Synopsis

The headline is the very <u>FIRST</u> thing someone will see. If your headlines fail to grab the attention of your readers, it doesn't matter how good your offer is or how good the rest of your copy is.

You only have 3 to 5 seconds to make an impact on your readers before they move on, so you need to make it count.

Here's an example of some good, time-tested headlines provided by DigitalMarketer:

Social Proof Headlines

- ✓ Here is a Method That is Helping [world class example] to [blank]
- ✓ [blank] Hacking With [world class example]
- ✓ Savvy|Smart|Sexy People Do XYZ
- ✓ Why I [blank] (And Maybe You Should Too)
- ✓ [Do something] like [world-class example]
- ✓ The [desired result] That [world class example] Is Talking About
- ✓ Join [impressive number] of Your Peers that [take desired action]
- ✓ [desired result] Like A [desired group or person]
- ✓ How [impressive number] Got [desired result] in [time period]
- ✓ Like [world class example] You Can [desired result]
- ✓ [world class example] Reveals Ways To [desired result]
  Why [impressive number] of People are [taking desired action]
- ✓ A Simple Way To [desired result] That Works For [desired group/person]
- ✓ How to [desired result] Like [world class example]

Threat Headlines

- ✓ Do You Recognize the [number] Early Warning Signs of [blank]?
- ✓ If You Don't [blank] Now, You'll Hate Yourself Later

- ✓ I've Lied to You for [time period] Now
- ✓ The Biggest Lie In [your industry]
- ✓ X Shocking Mistakes Killing Your [blank]
- ✓ Don't Try [blank] Without [desired action] First
- ✓ [blank] May Be Dangerous To [something precious]
- ✓ [blank] May Be Causing You To Lose Out On [desired result]
- ✓ At Last, The Secret To [desired result] Is Revealed
- ✓ The [blank] Risk Hiding In Your [blank]
- ✓ Why you shouldn't [do what I desire them to do]
- ✓ Why [blank] Fails and [blank] Succeeds
- ✓ Do Not Try Another [blank] Until You [take desired action]
- ✓ The Ugly Truth About [blank]
- ✓ What Your [blank] Won't Tell You And How It Can Save You [blank]
- ✓ What Everybody Ought to Know About [blank]
- ✓ Your [blank] Doesn't Want You To Read This [blank]
- ✓ The Sooner You Know [blank] The Better

Gain Headlines

- ✓ Where [desired result] Is And How To Get It
- ✓ Discover The [desired result] Secret
- ✓ [blank] Your Way To A [desired result] You

- ✓ To People That Want To [desired result] But Can't Get Started
- ✓ You, a [desired result]
- ✓ Stop [undesired result]
- ✓ You Too Can [desired result] in [time period] with [blank]
- ✓ How To Become [desired result] When You [something challenging]
- ✓ There's Big [desired result] In [blank]
- ✓ You Don't Have to Be [something challenging] to be [desired result]
- ✓ Little Known Ways to [blank]
- ✓ How to turn [blank] into [desired result]
- ✓ How To Build a [blank] You Can Be Proud Of
- ✓ Get [desired result] Without [undesired result]
- ✓ Get Rid of [problem] Once and For All
- ✓ Improve/Increase Your [desired result] In [time period]
- ✓ Imagine [desired result] And Loving Every Minute Of It
- ✓ Here's a Quick Way to [solve a problem]
- ✓ Get [desired result] Without Losing [blank]
- ✓ The Lazy [blank's] Way to [desired result]
- ✓ How To Make People Line Up And Beg To [blank]
- ✓ How To Get [desired result] Out Of [blank]

- ✓ How To [desired result] When You're Not [blank]
- ✓ No [undesired result] Just [desired result] Everyday
- ✓ Never Suffer From [undesired result] Again
- ✓ The Quickest & Easiest Way To [desired result]
- ✓ If You Can [blank] You Can [desired result]
- ✓ How You Can [desired result] Almost Instantly
- ✓ How To Become [desired result] When You [something challenging]
- ✓ How To Use [blank] To [desired result]
- ✓ How To Turn Your [blank] Into [desired result]
- ✓ See How Easily You Can [desirable result]
- ✓ Now You Can Have [something desirable] Without [something challenging]
- ✓ How To Take The Headache Out Of [blank]
- ✓ X Questions Answered About [blank]
- ✓ Give Me [short time period] and I'll Give You [desired result]
- ✓ Answered: Your Most Burning Questions About [blank]
- ✓ Take X minutes to get started with [blank]... you'll be happy you did!
- ✓ Who Else Wants [desired result]?
- ✓ How to fast-track your [desirable result]
- ✓ How [impressive number] Got [desired result] Without [undesired result]

Here's an important thing to note: You should never use FULL caps for your headline. Only use it when necessary.

"IMAGINE WHAT THIS WOULD LOOK LIKE IF THIS WAS ON THE TOP OF YOUR WEBPAGE!!!"

It looks like someone screaming at you – Who would like that? Also, full caps looks spammy and nobody nor Google would like that.

Also, headlines have to use eye-catching words which can **instantly excite** the emotions. Have you ever seen magazines at a newsstand?

Especially the tabloids?

The headlines usually sound catchy and use words which bring out curiosity and strike emotions with topics like sex, money and drama.

Ask yourself, what niche are you in? What words can you use to push emotions and create drama in your niche?

Many times, with drama, comes attention and with attention comes money.

Think about it... want to keep a conversation interesting?

Add drama to it (and to the relationship/friendship).

This isn't life advice but it will definitely heat things up a bit and strike emotions rarely touched.

Do this correctly... and you'll be *shocked* by the response you receive.

Chapter 4:

USP vs. ESP

Synopsis

We talked a lot about emotions in the previous chapter. Back in the "good old days," many businesses use something called "Unique Selling Point" or "Unique Selling Propositions" to differentiate themselves from their competitors to rake in more sales.

And that worked...for a while.

But if you're not paying attention to ESP... you're leaving a lot of money on the table and a lot of website visitors, unconverted.

Which One Do You Focus ON?

While USP's are very important, in the online world, we have something additional called "Emotional Selling Point's."

This is the ability subtly tap into the emotions of your readers so that you can make them carry out your most desired action.

Here's an example of an emotional selling point:

"I know what it's like struggling as a new entrepreneur, banging your head against the computer, trying to learn how to profitably drive traffic to your website.

At one point, it got so bad for me, I was scrounging through the couch, desperate to find a few lose pieces of change that I could use to buy a .50 cent bag of Ramon Noodles for dinner while hoping for one of my ads to convert.

This classic example targets *new* entrepreneurs and relates to them with a story of common hardships the reader is probably currently facing.

Emotional selling points also deal a lot with powerful emotion stimulating words.

For example, in the make money online niche, you would use words like: *"time and financial freedom, free yourself from the shackles of a 9-5, quit the rat face, fire your boss".*

These terms are ***emotional* terms** related to the niche that people can easily relate to and connect with. In short, if you want to use ESPs effectively to market your business, ask yourself these two questions:

1) What niche are you in?
2) What kind of words/stories/situations that people in your niche can identify with?

Once you have determined the answer to these two questions, you can try and brainstorm as many ESPs as possible that you can use in your sales copies or marketing content.

Another tip is to research your niche on Amazon.

Look for a book that has hundreds of reviews, then, read those reviews and get a REAL understand of what your target market is *feeling*.

Even negative feedback could be repurposed a an "objection obliterator".

Again, this is what your target is **ACTUALLY** thinking so pay close attention to their feedback.

It could be the very information that turns your promotion into a million-dollar winner.

Chapter 5:

Call To Action

Synopsis

The call to action is one of the most critical components of any piece of content. The first thing you need to do is determine what your most desired outcome is that you wish for your customers/prospects to carry out.

Action

Different components of your business would usually require a different sort of desired outcome.

For example…

- ✓ Blog – Comments
- ✓ Facebook page – Likes/Shares
- ✓ Landing page – Opt ins
- ✓ Emails – Click throughs
- ✓ Sales pages – Purchases

These are the *common* types of results you would typically want.

So once you have determined that, your call to action must be worded or shaped to facilitate that kind of action.

For example: For a blog setting, a good call to action would be – "If you liked this post or have any ideas of your own, please comment down below!"

As silly as it may sound to *literally* tell a reader what to do, split test studies have shown this to be really effective. The best way to achieve results fast is to model what others have been doing which works and eliminates things that don't work!
To give another example… if you want your prospects to make a purchase, you might ask them to "Snatch up your copy before it runs out!"

Note that I've added a simple scarcity factor (one of the extra marketing nuggets often used) by claiming that it will run out if you don't act now.

Adding scarcity factors or time sensitivity to your call to actions often result in high conversions, so don't forget to include it in whatever you do!

Finally, you need to remember that the success rate of the call to action is not solely the result of the words of use in the calling, but how you put together different components of your sales copy such as ESPs, handling objections and showing the benefits.

Chapter 6:

Handling Objections

Synopsis

Handling objections is a mandatory skill every copywriter must have. Otherwise they are effectively *sterile* as copywriters.

Objections

Whenever a person reads a piece of sales copy, questions will pop up in their mind in attempt to "protect" them from "losing their money".

This is a natural behavior, and if you know how to handle these objections effectively in your copy as they emerge, you'll reap massive rewards.

Here are a couple commonly used techniques for handling objections:

1) Testimonials

Social proof is something almost everyone looks for when they want to buy a product. The more convincing and authentic the testimonial seems, the more they will believe the product is good. Try to include testimonials with snapshots of the buyer, or use video testimonials if possible to appear more genuine.

Late night penis pill commercials do this like skilled assassins.

After providing tons of interview style testimonials, they then say something like...

"Over 1 million people have purchased XYZ pill, they can't all be wrong"

2) FAQS

Having a frequently asked questions section helps greatly in overcoming any objections that appear. This has become common in the JVzoo.com and Clickbank.com sales letters you see today (2016-2017).

Here you can address all the common misconceptions that may rise up.

Things like, how to use the product, who the product right for, are their any upsells coming up and price concerns.

3) Post scripts (P.S)

P.S or Post scripts have been used extensively in sales letters to boost conversions. Before clicking the "Add To Cart" button people will usually have a final line of defense which prevents them from making the purchase. If you have a couple of post scripts ready, you can give them that final nudge to make the purchase.

4) Good reasons to buy

A personal favorite of mine, this section gives your readers a couple of good reasons to help them rationalize their purchase and greatly boost your profits.

Incorporate these great tools for handling objections in your copy and you'll soon see a spike in your sales!

Chapter 7:

Copywriting Mistakes To Avoid

Synopsis

Everyone makes mistakes in their marketing career. This section aims to help you bypass the whole "experimental phase" and avoid the biggest mistakes ever made in copywriting.

Errors

Mistake #1: Selling before first demonstrating value

Before you blast your subscribers with offers, you must always give them loads of free value and establish a genuine relationship with them.

Mistake #2: Wrong text alignment

As a general rule of thumb, words should always be aligned to the left, indented inside slightly and not have too long a word line. This is to prevent a break in the continuity of your visitor's reading flow. (from left to right)

Also, images should be used sparingly, better graphics CAN improve sales, but only if its directly relevant to what you're writing and compliments the copy.

Mistake #3: Sounding too formal

Let's face it, if your pitch sounds too formal, you'll come off as sounding like a sales robot. For crying out loud, throw in some human factor and speak with a casual tone.

No one likes to be hard sold, so if you can connect with your readers in a more informal tone, they'll identify with you and you'll be more likely to make that sale.

Mistake #4: Wasting your reader's time

Basically, to write good copy, you should only be adding things which contribute to the sale and removing things which do not. Your reader's attention is very precious.

That means, if you manage to catch their attention, make it count. Don't *bore* them with useless stuff just because you think it sounds *cute, cool, nifty, rhymes or funny.*

In short, if you avoid these mistakes and diligently practice copywriting methods as shown above, you'll get better and better in no time and make more sales.

<u>There is no magic pill.</u>

No magic book, course or software will ever replace an A-List copywriter (or even a B-List one) who has put in the work to TEST their copy and PROVE they know what they are doing.

However, if you do get the many software's available...

... they **CAN** be a great tool for teaching you formula's and *reasons why* the software *did what it did.*

Here's the deal: At the end of the day, you don't have to be the BEST copywriter in the world to make money, you just need to be better than the other guy in town (if you're local).

And if you're online, you can find traffic for pennies on the dollar and run traffic to a blog post, then drive those folks to an affiliate offer.

In fact, that might be the *best* way to start your path on learning how to write *converting* copy.

Don't know how to set up a simple blog to write these posts?

It's okay, most folks don't when they start out.

That's why they use freelance/outsource website's like:

- ✓ Upwork.com
- ✓ Freelancer.com
- ✓ Guru.com
- ✓ Fiverr.com

Chapter 8:

Swipe Files

Synopsis

This section deals with swipe files that you can instantly use to improve your sales copy. These swipe files aren't meant to be directly stolen and ripped word for word.

In fact, to prevent that kinda crapola, I've included my personal pieces of copy which are only the first (or second) drafts of the final piece.

Why have I done this?

Actually, there are 2 *very* specific reasons...

Reason #1: I wanted to make sure that any slimeball villain directly copying these swipes word for word has only moderate chances of success

And...

Reason #2: If you want to learn the fundamentals of copy, then study the way the copy was written

The words might change but the psychology very *rarely* does.

That's why you don't copy shit word for word, simply use it as a tool to learn from.

These swipes are essentially "idea generators" to write your own copy, based on winning principles.

Use These Different Kinds Swipes For Mega Profits =>

Email 1-

Subject: Here are the Sample Advertorials you requested…

Hey <firstname>,

I appreciate your interest in getting an Advertorial written for your company.

As promised, I've included multiple samples of some our Advertorials in this email.

And as you'll discover, they're for *different* niches and what's better is, they're ***all*** converting.

One of the biggest things we pride ourselves on is having the top writers and market researchers in the world working with us side-by-side to ensure you get a *targeted* advertorial…

…Which *actually* converts your readers and makes them click over to your page to learn more.

Once you go over these samples, head over to our page and get started with one of our "done for you" packages.

Get Your Professional Advertorial Written Now >>>

To Higher Conversions,

Signature

P.S. Also, if you're not getting the conversions we promised you, **you'll get all your money back.**

That means, it either wins and converts (8 out of 10 of our advertorials convert)… or it doesn't and you don't spend a dime.

Email 2-

Subject: 15% to 25% conversion rates?

Hey <firstname>,

Did you get a chance to check out the samples?

The reason we've had over 1000 people show interest in our service is because we've been running "native-ads" since 2011.

And since then, we've invested over $1.6 million of our own money, into sending traffic to our ads so we can test them.

That means, we've made all the mistakes and errors most people do when trying to make their Advertorial convert.

And the best part is, we've developed a special framework which gets our clients *consistent* results.

In fact, our own sites will typically get anywhere between a 20% to 25% conversion rate.

And most of our clients get 10% to 15% conversion (if they follow our advice).

That's from the Advertorial to the destination page.

These results are *rare* for many companies and it's part of why our clients love working with us and why you will also.

We're interested in building a long-term, profitable relationship with you and appreciate your business.

Simply click on the link below and choose one of our 2 Advertorial Packages.

Get Your Professional Advertorial Written Now >>>

To Higher Conversions,

Signature

P.S. Remember, if for some reason our ads *don't* convert, you'll get an automatic refund on all your money.

The last thing we want to do is leave you "high and dry" with something that doesn't work.

Click over to the next page and let's get started!

Email 3-

Subject: Professional company vs Freelancer writers?

Hey <firstname>,

Have you ever hired a freelancer who works on your advertorials, websites, marketing or anything else?

If you have, then you might relate to what I'm about to say.

You see, many times, freelancers (regardless of the industry) have an "eat what you kill" mentality.

And although that's great for getting new business, it's *terrible* when trying to build a long-term, sustainable,
"win-win" relationship.

The thing is, when you're getting your advertorial written, you need an *expert* who understands your *niche* and industry.

And more importantly, you need someone who knows how to position your company as a leading authority and deliver results.

That's what we do for you.

We're with you every step of the way and if for some reason the advertorial we write for you *doesn't* convert, we'll give you all your money back.

The goal is to get you conversions!

Click over to get started and choose from one of our 2 Advertorial Packages.

We'll do it right for you, the first time!

To Higher Conversions,

Signature

P.S. One of the biggest benefits of working with a legitimate company, rather than a "fly by night" freelancer, is you have real professionals.

Professionals who have all the resources needed to really make your "native ad" a home-run success!

Email 4-

Subject: The 3000 year old winning Ad formula...

Hey <firstname>,

Many times, prospective clients ask how we're able to write for virtually any market.

The answer is simple.

You see, we've developed a systematic process which almost always gets conversions for our clients.

The reason why is because after investing over $1.6 million in sending traffic to our own ads, we've discovered a formula which has consistently created wins for us.

And the best part is, when we rolled it out to clients, it *still* consistently created wins.

That's why we opened this new company.

Our winning formula and massive amounts of testing gives us a competitive advantage over all the freelance copywriters.

In fact, it's the same competitive advantage that YOU get to benefit from directly when you have us write your advertorial.

I do have a confession though...

See, this formula wasn't *entirely* created by us.

A lot of our insider strategies are actually inspired by a 3,000 year old "Greek Persuasion Formula" we discovered while studying Socrates.

In his book, "On Rhetoric" he dives into detail about 3 simple elements which he called Ethos, Pathos,
Logos...

...And they could be used to persuade almost anyone while sounding like a trustful advisor.

It's our secret to crafting winning advertorials in extremely diverse markets.

You see, when these 3 elements were put into action – It would allow *anyone* to present on *any* topic and *still* appear trustworthy.

Socrates then also outlined a presentation delivery framework, commonly called the P.A.S. method today.

The P.A.S. method is used by top copywriters all over the world.

The reason it's so effective is because **it leverages human psychology which *no* human can resist.**

It sucks them right into your message and compels them to act immediately.

We combined the P.A.S. method with a bit of Neurolinguistics Programming (NLP) along with the Ethos, Pathos, Logos elements to create a "fail-proof" writing system.

The combination consistently churned out advertorials which beat our controls.

On top of that, we've also formatted a 10-Step process to ensure every one of our clients gets a great experience.

You can check it out by going to the link below:

<Insert link to pricing page>

To Higher Conversions,

Signature

P.S. There's no other company around which will give you all your money back if the Advertorial doesn't convert.

We Will.

The reason we're so confident is because after testing these ads since before 2011 and after investing 7-figures into driving traffic to them for ourselves...

...We know what works and even *more* importantly, ***what doesn't.***

Click over to check out our 2 available options and see for yourself!

Email 5-

Subject: If it doesn't work, you pay NOTHING...

Hey <firstname>,

Have you had a chance to review the samples I sent over a few days ago?

We've had so many people contacting us for advertorials and there's a really good reason for it!

You see, on top of having the best writers, researchers and persuasion *system*, we're also the only company willing to put their money where their mouth is.

That means, when you hire us to write your Ad, we'll make sure it has the absolute *highest* chances of converting.

And if it doesn't?

Simple.

You get ALL your money back.

Listen, I'm okay with taking all the risk.

After doing this for so many years, investing over $1.6 million in driving traffic to test our own advertorials…

…And simplifying everything into a step-by-step system which has been proven to work over and over again – We've discovered that when we work with clients, they see results **8 out of 10 times.**

That means, for every 10 people we work with, 2 will get their money back.

This definitely isn't the goal, it's just the statistics.

That's why we're able to make such an incredible offer where you pay nothing, if our ads don't work.

The worst thing that could happen is we work together, run an ad which doesn't work, and you get your money back.

And even then, it still gives you a "no cost" test where you get to see what your prospects ***aren't*** responding to…

…Making your next ad even better (whether you go with us or not).

If you'd like to get started with your Advertorial today, simply click on the link below to choose your package.

Get Your Professional Advertorial Written Now >>>

To Higher Conversions,

Signature

P.S. There's no other company in the world which will give you all your money back if the Advertorial they write doesn't convert.

We Will.

Your happiness and success with our service is our ultimate goal and we pride ourselves on getting BIG results for our clients.

Click over to the next page and let's get started!

How to increase your SEO rankings, crank up your website to lightning speeds and effortlessly increase your income...

Your Website Is Repelling Visitors Without You Even Knowing It

<Insert Autoplay VSL>

You're about to discover:

- ✓ The #1 reason visitors go to your site and **INSTANTLY** back out (not what you might think)
- ✓ How to convert more sales on your website *without* changing a single word (this is a game-changer)
- ✓ Secret strategy used by CNN, Yahoo and other multi-million dollar companies (If it's worked for them, maybe it'll work for you too?)
- ✓ And much, *much* more!

<Make Buy Button and Guarantee Copy Pop Up At The Close of The Video, this is a timed-delay>

Dear Friend,

I remember slapping the side of my laptop... hoping to make my website load faster.

Obviously... ***it didn't work.***

The thing is, the load time on my website was so slow, it was actually *repelling* visitors.

I didn't think much of it at first but after checking my stats, I noticed my sales were WAY down.

Why?

Simple – people were *trying* to visit my site, but since it took so long to load…
… they quickly backed out and went somewhere else.

This is more common than you might think.

In fact, it's why big companies like CNN and Yahoo use the same strategy I'm about to show you to make their websites **rank better** with SEO and instantly load at lightning speeds.

See, when you have a website that takes forever to load, it kills any SEO efforts your spending time and money on.

What's worse is, it'll start driving your revenue down the drain.

That means, if you're website isn't running at optimal speeds, 24/7, you are essentially shooting yourself in the foot and working *backwards.*

The crazy thing is, you might not even know how much damage your site is taking on due to the slow loading time.

The truth is, if you're not seeing very many sales from your website currently, chances are good that it's because it's loading poorly.

There are 2 primary reasons for this…

REASON #1: The code and database of your website isn't optimized in the right way and things aren't where they need to be

And…

REASON #2: You may have a slow server or you aren't using a Content Delivery Network (CDN)

"Great… So What Can I Do About This?"

Like I said, I've experienced this first hand and it's almost crippled my business. It got so bad, I felt like I was just throwing money away when I tried doing SEO or Facebook Ads.

Nothing converted.

At first I thought maybe it was the copy, or even my traffic.

But it wasn't.

After spending hours banging my head against the wall, trying my best to figure out what the heck was going on... I finally did it!

Once my website's speed was super-fast, sales started to trickle in again.

Thankfully, I was able to discover the **real problem** behind the lack of sales.

The good thing is, you won't have to do all of the hard work I did though.

Nope.

You won't need to spend hours or *even days* binging on coffee and Adderall, trying to make your website load faster.

Here's why...

After years of owning our own websites and relying on them as our sole sources of income, my friend Satish and I have combined forces and put together WP Speedy PRO.

WP Speedy PRO is a simple Wordpress Plugin that automatically does all the hard work for you and gives your Wordpress site a turbo boost.

There's **no coding, analyzing or "figuring things out"** – with this revolutionary new plugin, you're able to easily plug and play.

Simply, sit back and let WP Speedy PRO do all the heavy lifting for you.
While you're relaxing, doing other work or simply watching T.V., here's what WP Speedy PRO is doing for you:

1. **Magnification and Optimization -** Once You Install WP Speedy PRO, it will minify and optimize your JAVASCRIPT, CSS, Database & Images without interfering with anything... This makes your website to load at lightning speeds

2. **CDN Service -** Next, the WP Speedy PRO will make copies of your static files such as your theme's css, javascript , icons, images and put it into **152 different** servers around the globe

3. **Faster Load Time -** When a visitor comes to your website, WP Speedy PRO will pull static content from multiple servers nearest to the visitor, which

will load the website almost instantly because there are multiple connections, rather than just one connection trying to fulfill the requests of all the visitors

Pretty crazy, huh?

Essentially, WP Speedy PRO makes your life *easier* and your website visitors love you.

In fact, they'll love you so much, some will even buy from you!
Here's a quick demo video of how it works…

<Insert Demo Video>

Here's What People Are Saying About WP Speedy PRO

<Insert Testimonial>
<Insert Testimonial>
<Insert Testimonial>
<Insert Testimonial>
<Insert Testimonial>

As you can see, this plugin has helped a lot of folks just like you speed up their website, increase sales and transform their life.

This isn't magic or voodoo though.

It might feel like that at first (because of the results you'll see), but it's a scientific approach towards increasing your income.

In fact, on top of making your website load faster, you'll also start to notice…

- ✓ You'll spend less time trying to fix your websites bugs and issues
- ✓ **You'll start earning more income because *more* visitors are able to access your website**
- ✓ You'll start growing an **organic** following because WP Speedy PRO helps your SEO rankings by keeping your code clean and website fast
- ✓ **And much, *much* more!**

How Much Is WP Speedy PRO?

WP Speedy PRO was originally going to sell for $497.

And why not?

It's worth **every single penny**.

Just think about it, if you were able to attract thousands of visitors to your website and convert **MORE** of those visitors because of your load time, you could *easily* make back the $497.

But this won't cost that much.

In fact, it won't even cost half of that.

For the next X <insert launch days> days only, you'll have the opportunity to invest in WP Speedy PRO for **pennies on the dollar.**

To make it even better, you can use it on up to 5 domains!

Which of these 2 plans works better for you?

Plan #1 – You can access WP Speedy PRO for only $27 per year

Or...

Plan #2 – This is the most popular option, you can save 42% and access WP Speedy PRO for only $47, renewed every 3 years

This offer won't be up for long though.

If you want WP Speedy PRO, you need to **ACT NOW** and order immediately.

30-Day No Wiesel Clause, Money-Back Guarantee

If for ANY reason (or no reason), you feel like WP Speedy PRO hasn't delivered on everything I just said, simply return it within 30 days for a full, 100% refund.

No questions asked. No hard feelings.

Listen, life is too short to have bad karma lurking over my shoulder, so if you aren't pleased with WP Speedy PRO, I don't want you to pay for it.

That means, this is totally **RISK-FREE** for you and you have nothing to lose.

I know you won't want a refund though.

I'm confident you'll start seeing *predictable* results, just like these folks did…

<Insert 5 testimonials>

Getting started is *easy*.

Simply click on the link below to order immediately.

I promise, this will be the best decision you ever make.

Plus, it's totally **RISK-FREE** so you have nothing to lose and literally everything to gain.

Make sure you do this right now though, before anything else pops up on your computer.

This is a digital age, with a lot of digital distractions.

Right now, there's really only 3 options for you to choose from…

Option #1: You can take everything I just shared with you on this page and say, "thanks but no thanks" and go back to your normal life, with your slow website, normal sales and normal bank account.

Option #2: You can take what you learned, dabble a little "here and there" and hopefully see some kind results in your load-time, based on your trial and error.

Or

Option #3: This is the most popular option. You can skip past all the hard work, leap-frog to the front of the line and use the "done for you" WP Speedy PRO plugin to instantly speed up your website so it can start earning more money, right away!

I would choose option 3 if I were you… it's **RISK-FREE** and you literally have **NOTHING** to lose.

So choose your Plan right now and click the button on this page to get started immediately!

To Faster Loading Times,

Vas Majority and Satish Gaire

<make this section below look like a coupon with a checkbox they can click, insert 30 day guaranteed symbol>

Yes! I want to dramatically increase the load time of my website and improve my rankings on Google. I understand that if I dislike WP Speedy PRO for any reason whatsoever, I can get all of my money back by taking advantage of the 30 day money back guarantee.

<Insert 2 buy button options with paypal and verification symbols>

<INSERT FAQ Section>

Q: Is WP Speedy Pro a monthly recurring service to use the system?
A: No, there are no monthly commitments. Your investment is a yearly or tri-yearly one-time fee and you can use it for as long as your website stands!

Q: Do you provide customer support for WP Speedy PRO
A: Of course! Our friendly support team are available if you need any help with using WP Speedy PRO.

Q: What are the requirements to using WP Speedy PRO?
A: All you need is WordPress installed on your website. Installing WP Speedy PRO is easy and takes seconds to install.

Q: Do I need a special theme to use this plugin or can I use it on our normal WordPress site?
A: This is a powerful plugin that works with virtually all WP themes.

FINALLY! How you can get the #1 Women's Fitness Product On Amazon... *FREE*

Will He Still Look At You The Same?

80% Of The Battle Is Just Hitting "Play" On The DVD Player

Here's a simple way you can SLASH your long and boring workouts into just 3 "Belly-Busting", 30 minute sessions per week ...And how you can get started FREE

Dear Friend,

I have a confession.

You see, I was the kind of girl who bought fitness DVDs with the best of intentions.

I got the DVD and all of the recommended props, cleared a special space out in my spare room and got all fired up to get fit at home.

I would dive into the first few workouts with the kind of zeal usually reserved only for freedom fighters.

I was like- "I am going to be SO IN SHAPE, guys!"

Then... *nothing.*

The thing is, I'd get bored. I'd get lonely. I'd crave the energy and atmosphere of a real life gym or yoga class.

And there they'd sit, in the corner, collecting dust...

P90X, Insanity. 30-Day Shred. And - I'm not kidding you here - the ENTIRE catalog of Crunch and Gaiam DVDs.

These were all sad and depressing examples of my willpower.

After having 2 kids of my own, I decided to do something.

So, I became obsessed with "Women Specific" fitness and health, taking every course and studying every aspect of the female body and how it could *safely* burn fat... fast.

I was obsessed with finding the "holy grail" of fitness products.

You see, It seemed as if nothing "out there" actually spoke to me.
Nothing spoke to moms like us who had just left the hospital and discovered that we still looked pregnant.

And still needed to wear our maternity clothes, even *after* having our baby.

You know what?

I *found* that "hard to find" program and I'm now one of the Co-Founders of the company.

It's called FeFit.

This program is designed specifically for moms and women generally over 30 years old.

It'll show you step-by-step every kind of "weird" little-known exercise trick that has been discovered to be *highly* effective.

And you know what?

It works like crazy!

So crazy that it even ended up being the #1 Women's Fitness Product on Amazon!

I have women and mothers emailing me <u>daily</u> about how their husbands are looking at them more and showing them *a lot* more attention.

They tell me that since getting on my FeFit program, their husbands are even more impressed by the effort they put forth in making a positive change in their body.

Here's the thing though…

You might even start having trouble going out to the grocery store without a guy trying to talk to you, hoping you're available.

So if that's uncomfortable to you, just make sure you dress a little less revealing.

Once you start seeing results, you'll notice yourself packing away the maternity clothes and wanting to wear different kinds of clothing.

You'll be wearing more dresses, skirts, shorts, etc.

And that's OK!

In fact, it's perfectly normal.

You are a beautiful woman who deserves to be desired

Right?

Of course!

Just keep in mind that you'll also be effortlessly attracting members of the opposite gender.

So just pay attention to what you're wearing ;).

You see, the entire package is a 13-Week FeFit Bootcamp that will whip your body into amazing shape without the boring same old workouts repeated over and over again.

I know this 13-Week workout will work wonders on you, and I know that once you *watch the First DVD,* you'll be addicted and want to get the whole package.

That's why I've put together a really awesome special offer just for you

You can get the 1st Intro DVD of my 13-Week FeFit Bootcamp for **FREE** plus a whopping $7 ($12 if you're international) for shipping and handling.

This is like "dipping your toe in the water" before jumping right in

And you see, there's absolutely NO sneaky bait and switch tactics here.

I hate those things and think anyone using them to sell their products should be thrown in jail for at least 25 years.

The reason I'm basically *giving this away* to you is because I know that once you watch this **first DVD**, you'll want to go ahead and *grab everything else I have.*

I've also made sure to provide easy-to-follow guidance and instruction, packed with A LOT OF MOTIVATION and even made ALL the workouts scalable so it doesn't matter what level you're at...

... I'll have a workout just for you and your fitness level

This is totally risk-free and I want to make sure I earn your business and more importantly, *your trust.*

Without that, I can't grow my business and reach my dream of providing fitness to all the mothers going through after- pregnancy weight loss challenges.

I also believe in Karma and know that by giving you the opportunity to "test-drive" my program for only the cost of shipping, you'll return the favor by getting all my stuff and telling all your friends.

[Button To Pay]

Here's a promise I'll make you...

When you get this **FREE DVD**, obviously you'll leap into your usual patterns.

You'll be super motivated. You'll tell all of your friends, urging them to buy the set so you can work out "together", but separately.
In your own houses.

And despite your outward excitement, you might still have underlying feelings of preemptive guilt, knowing this too will soon join your own personal Island of **"Lonely Exercise DVDs"** that never get used more than *once*.

But then something magical will happen

After putting in the 1st DVD you get from me, you'll actually *enjoy* your first FeFit workout.

And the next one. And the next one. And the next one after that.

You see...

It will be challenging

And that's *good.*

But what's even better is, you'll join my online support group and you'll love the people in it– they'll feel like old friends and fulfill your need to be social during a workout.

And the availability of different workouts, combined with the short workout duration, will keep you interested and actually looking forward to your next FeFit workout day.

The major aspect of FeFit that you'll really appreciate is the active social media community.

The engagement will actually help to keep you motivated and connected to the other women in the community just like you, kinda like we're all on the same journey together.

[Button To Pay]

Cheesy? Maybe. But hey... whatever keeps you interested

Right?

Bottom line – If you're looking for a challenging workout routine that won't suck hours and hours out of your week, yet still whips your lazy butt into shape... THIS IS IT.

And, if you really want to have some fun, ask your significant other to join you. Laugh when he scoffs at doing a "women's workout."

Then laugh again when he gives out halfway through the DVD.

You're welcome.

Here's some of what you'll be getting and experiencing...

- **Each workout is completely different** so you won't be bored and neither will your muscles and body! I know that keeping interested is one of the biggest factors to actually losing weight. If you're not interested, you're not committed. And if you're not committed, you'll never see results. I make sure you're interested, enthusiastic and FULLY COMMITTED so you see REAL results

- **If you're short on time, you will love that the Fe Fit program** only requires 30 minutes a day, 3-4 days a week. This is the amount of time each of us should workout in a week anyway, but if you can't stand long hour long workouts, you will love how quickly the 30 minute workout goes by!

- **You'll discover brand new moves you've never even done before** to target some MAJOR problem areas! This program provides you with a lot of variety. You'll even find cardio, stretch, and barre workouts on these DVDs.

- **You'll love that there is a fitness level for everyone, but you will be amazed at how much of a good workout you get out of these**

videos. It's easy to work up a sweat with these DVDs and you'll feel sore after almost every workout you do, even if you consider yourself in pretty good shape! Again, if you're a beginner and this intimidates you, don't worry! With each move, I'll also give you a modified version so it is easier for you to do, until your muscles can adjust and you can work your way up to the moderate level or *even the more advanced level!*

- **You can also save yourself a ton of money by forgoing the gym membership**, and you won't need expensive fitness equipment to do this program either! 30 minutes a day, 3 times a week, is all you need to achieve the body of your dreams!

- **After just 2 weeks on the program you'll be more than happy with it**. Although I can't say "happy" is the best word. Because the exercises are exhausting, these workouts push your endurance and burn your muscles. Down the road, I'm sure "happy" will be a good fit. But right now, let's stick with "challenging." Challenging in a good way. You will be challenged for your own good and you WILL see results

Getting started with your FREE FeFit DVD is simple.

Just fill out the box on the top right of this page.

[Button To Pay]

Once you complete your order, we will send out your DVD the SAME DAY, you'll also be able to instantly stream the first DVD within minutes after purchase so you can "dive in" right away *without waiting*.

3 Guarantees You Can Bet The Farm On

GUARANTEE#1 – First and foremost, I guarantee that if you're unhappy with the purchase, even a little bit, I will fully refund your $7 *(or 12 if international),* no questions asked. No hard feelings.

GUARANTEE #2 – I Guarantee that you will LOVE the online support group we have and everyone in there! Building friendships even *across the world*.

GUARANTEE #3 – I Guarantee to always provide the most cutting-edge and highly-effective weight loss techniques dedicated *specifically* to mothers wanting to lose the "baby fat" after pregnancy.

Order your **FREE DVD** right now and I'll make sure this is the *wisest* investment in your health that you ever make.

[Button To Pay]

To Your Happiness and Weight Loss

Signature

P.S. Order your copy right now and share it with a friend! Remember, when you order now, you'll also be able to get it streamed onto your computer within MINUTES!

Order now and fill out the form on the top right of this website!

P.P.S. Check out what some of our Amazon customers are saying about this...

<Insert Testimonials>

"Anti-Social Sales Veteran Spills The Beans And Reveals His Proven 7-Figure Closing Secrets"

On this page you'll discover...

- ✓ **The Closely-Guarded Sales Secrets Of 4 MASTER Closers**
- ✓ **How To *Ethically* Hack Into Your Prospects Mind And Understand What They *Really* Want (it's not what you might think)**
- ✓ **How To Make The Phone Your Most Profitable Asset**
- ✓ **The "Dork-Proof" Method For Closing Deals (even if you suck at phone sales)**
- ✓ **The Difference Between "Closing" and "Yapping"**
- ✓ **How To Quickly Skyrocket Your Closing Rate – Guaranteed**
- ✓ **And Much, MUCH MORE!**

Dear Friend,

"Pick up the phone and start dialing!"

Something about being in a boiler room, phone room, sales floor … or whatever you want to call it, turns me on **and gets my "greed-glands" pumping faster than just about anything else.**

Why?

Because when I'm there, I know money is being made – especially when I'm surrounded by **top-dog closers** who've slugged it out, side-by-side with me, in the trenches, day-in and day-out.

You see, I got into sales because I had no other choice.

The truth is, there was no way I'd be able to get a job any place else, it just didn't fit who I was.

And after training literally hundreds, if not **THOUSANDS** of professionals… here's what I've discovered – most people get on the phone… ***and get scared.***

Like little puppies… all bark and no bite…

Even the ones who weren't scared and appeared to be *naturals,* ***even they*** had a hard time shutting down a deal.

Sure, they could open up a call and talk the prospects ear off… but when it came down to asking for the money…

…They just kinda *winged* it.

This made them *look* like naturals, but in reality, they were broke.

All of them.

Listen, here's what most people do when they try to sell stuff…

They pick up the phone, open their mouth and just start **YAPPING**!

Most of the time, they don't know what twists and turns are coming up.

They just start blabbing off and wonder why they can't get any results.

Just think about it…

It'd be like you getting in the car and saying, "I want to go somewhere but I don't know the address."

How are you going to get there?

I mean, you could *wing it* and just *hope* to get there… but you and I both know, *hope* isn't a very good plan for success.

Hey, my name is Eric Pathi.

I'm a master closer and have been retained by multi-million dollar companies to take over their entire sales department.

Anyone I train, and put through my system… can literally go from **zero to hero**, in no time flat.

You can be a total *dork*, but if you went through my training, forget about it… **you're golden.**

You see, I wound up getting into sales at a younger age because I had a deeper voice and when I did tele-marketing, my voice wouldn't crack…

…So since my voice didn't crack, I was able to **basically get on the phone and talk to people twice my age.**

And you know what happened?

They gave me money.

Simply because of my voice and *a few tricks* I picked up along the way.

These tricks worked so well, virtually everyone who got on the phone with me ended up closing.

That's when it hit me… "this is a gold mine!"

You see, when you're on the phone, and selling, you can be anyone you want to be and if you can follow a few simple steps, you can go from closing only a small handful of sales per week…

…To becoming a **master closer** who seals the deal ***with virtually anyone*** that gets on the phone.

Some people are born with the gift of sales and other aren't, but the beauty of this system is, when you follow the steps, it doesn't matter if you're a natural or not.

You just read the words, follow the steps and *close the damn deal!*

My guys do it every, single, day – like *clockwork.*

And let me tell you, some of them could barely talk when they came to me!

After being told over and over again by sales trainers, CEOs and business owners that my sales training is leaps and bounds above anyone else's out there…

… I knew I needed to share it with other sales people, business owners and entrepreneurs who might be struggling in sales.

See, it's okay if your struggling *right now*… it's NOT okay if you know there's a solution and do NOTHING about it.

That's why I created something that lets you do something about it right now to quickly **jump-start** your closing skills.

It's called: Anatomy of The Close

Anatomy of The Close is the #1 sales system right now.

It's currently being used by multi-million dollar companies, as well as top sales professionals and entrepreneurs, who want to close more deals, *more often.*

Here's what a few people just like you are already saying about this system…

<Insert 3 Testimonial Videos>

Here's what you're going to get in Anatomy of The Close:

- An Exclusive 4-Part "MoneyMind" interview series with myself and 3 other master trainers…

The other 3 trainers are:

Ted Landman who is considered the most respected name in phone sales over the past 30 years.

In certain inner circles, he's known as ***Mr. Old School*** because of his "cut to the close" tactics.

Then you'll get training from…

Konstantin Safir – "Kosty" as I know him, is a conversational persuasion specialist.

He is among the elite of phone sales, with ***over a decade*** of experience in shutting deals down and getting the sale.

After Konstantin, you'll get trained by…

Barry Kandel – Barry is an elite closer who breaks down how he's able to close 5 and 6-figure deals, all over the phone.

On top of that, you'll also get...

Private, member only access to a secret Facebook group where Barry, Ted, Kosty and myself, answer questions and give you "real-time" advice you can take action on right away to start closing more deals.

And what's better is, we're also giving you **3 BIG BONUSES 100% FREE** when you get Anatomy of The Close today.

They are...

BIG BONUES #1: "Pitch Domination Secrets" – this is where we are role playing pitches, to help you fully understand the content

BIG BONUES #2: "Objection Obliteration Tactics" so you know exactly what to say to diffuse ANY objection and turn it into a sale

And...

BIG BONUES #3: "One-Hitter Quitters" is where we role play simple 1-liners you can start using immediately, this is where most people fall flat on their face

Frankly, after going through this system, you'll be shocked by what you DIDN'T know.

Here's some of what you'll discover...

- **An 'off the radar' technique you can use to turn inbound customer service calls into upsells...** This technique is completely passive, undetectable, and drives more profit to your bottom-line
- **The A-B-C formula of how to** use old school tactics while leveraging new school technology

Listen, I'm a self-admitted gadget junky...

...But you'll have that 'ah-ha' moment when you hear how you can increase your conversions using the 'same ole pitch' but evolving your presentation using the latest and greatest technology... **trust me on this.**

I'll also show you ...

- **The 'blank check' method, a fool-proof method you can use to effortlessly trigger your prospects mind into seeing the end result… you desire.**

  When you apply this technique, you'll have the power to literally write your own pay check, thus, the term 'blank check'

- **How to put your prospect into a "buying mindset" so that the close becomes almost automatic**

- Inside these rare interviews YOU will discover a set of POWERFUL tactics you can use to trigger this "buying mindset"

- **The top 3 things you MUST avoid during the 'pitch' Do you want to close a 'high ticket' sale, I'm talking closes ranging $1k - $100k?**

  Then you'll need to know the three things you MUST avoid at all costs during a phone call with the client!

- **How to position your bonuses and control the perception of value – Most people fail on the phone because they lack the ability to demonstrate value**

- Imagine your prospect twisting your arm begging you: "Take my money!" That's what insiders call a soft-close… Inside I'll show YOU the "tell-tale signs" you must know. When you detect one of these "tells"… the close is almost unavoidable!

- **The reverse close, this strategy goes against everything you've ever learned…**

  …Call it counterintuitive but this strategy was responsible for a single $100,000 close in recent month! Imagine closing 6-figures, from just 1 sale.

- **Master the art of REALLY understanding your prospects needs, desires and wants…**

  … After you hear this, you'll understand how to translate what your client is really saying

- **Effortlessly slice through the "I can't afford it" objection like a piece of cake -**

  I'll show you how to logically justify the cost of your product or service without facing objection…

  …Trust me, the person you're pitching, will WANT to give you their money, without any arm-twisting or back and forth haggling

- **The BIG picture method… Boost value into the BIG picture by justifying your offer into their lifestyle and the end result…**

...Many times, your prospect will go from wanting your offer to NEEDING YOUR OFFER!

- Most closes depend on how targeted your prospects or leads are... When you get access to Anatomy of the Close, you'll discover how **I guarantee inbound leads are sizzling, red hot!**

Inside, I'll also I talk about **The Perfect Game Plan** and how you must execute it to get consistent results, every time.

You'll also discover...

- ... the importance of the cadence and tone of your voice
- **... how to leverage every call-in so you never let a prospect slip through the cracks**
- ... a simple trick you can use to instantly gain equity in a client by leveraging a 12 month deal
- **... how to increase the customer value and turn an angry or unhappy client into a sale**
- ... leveraging landmarks in the pitch
- **... the call back method, plant the close in the first 30 seconds and watch what happens next!**
- ... How to use a secret blackops technique in your close to get the credit card number without ever asking for it
- **Pro-level secrets on how to get your prospect to reveal their objections in the beginning stages of the pitch... Knowing your prospects objections lets you craft a laser targeted offer!**

One thing I've discovered is that it's **SUPER IMPORTANT** your prospect like you.

Inside Anatomy of the Close, you'll discover clever tactics you can use that almost forces your prospect to like you!

- **Discover the true SECRET to selling high ticket items – It's not what you think.** You must leverage your personality, life style, other factors ABOUT YOURSELF to attract your prospect to your product or service

- Using "InfoTainment" to control the conversation (this is a cool trick where you're informative and entertaining!)

- **How to bypass you prospects "mental red tape" and avoid adversity, dodge their disapproval, shake their suspicion, and steer clear of their uncertainty... This is a sure-fire way to boost your close rate!**

- Power profiling... how to extract your prospects likes, dislikes, financial situation, family situation, why they called, daily routine and much more (This is a stealthy technique you've probably never used)

- **I'll show you step by step, how to relate with your prospect and become best friends with them by the time you ask for the money**
(Trust me, after thousands of calls and pitches, when you practice this one, little known strategy, your prospect will become an almost guaranteed close!)

- Face it, at the end of the day... You're batting for your clients' attention – If you allow their mind to wonder or what I call "droning," you'll drastically increase your closing rate!

- **Extracting the truth method: When you understand this, your prospects will think you're a mind reader!**

- Effortlessly uncover your prospects real needs, goals, pains, previous experiences, and reasons for why they need you

- **You'll uncover the mental triggers you need to plant in your prospects mind in the first five minutes of the pitch!**

- Why you need to squash objections as quickly as possible. This is the #1 SECRET to closing five figure deals!

- **Inbound calls are THE BEST, yet there's a certain way to approach them, I'll show you how you should handle these calls to maximize your chance of closing the deal!**

- A simple "life hack" you MUST use to soften your prospect up and hypnotize them into "The Buyers Mindset" (This technique is very POWERFUL and must only be used for good!)

- **Many professionals have their heart skip a beat when the prospect says, "How much does it cost?" I'll show you how to side-step the objection, build value and get paid!**

- The CoreCombo- You'll know the exact questions I ask my prospects and clients to peel away their walls and get to their core issues... When you have these "go to" questions in your tool box, you'll see results overnight!

There's so much you're getting it's not even funny.

What you're about to discover is literally worth millions of dollars.

It's created millionaires and helped average, and below average sales people, become absolute **ROCKSTAR** closers.

After using this system, introverts who felt like they couldn't talk their way out of a paper bag were suddenly able to close 5 and 6 figure deals.

Extroverts who loved talking but just couldn't get the sale, were sealing deals faster than ever before.

They just needed a **proven game-plan** that walked them through the call, step-by-step.

How Much Is It All Going To Cost?

Anatomy of the Close was originally going to sell for $997 dollars, but because I want to get this in as many hands as possible, you can get it right now for only $297 bucks!

That means you're literally saving $700 dollars when you take action today.

That's a steal of a deal and the best part is, it's just a one-time investment in your future.

Listen, I remember seeing my sales people working to the bone and hammering out the phones without any real luck.

What made the difference?

The skills I showed them, which I want to show you, too.

There's virtually **NO LEARNING CURVE**, as soon as you get Anatomy of the Close, you can start using it, right away.

Heck, if you close even one prospect using these techniques, you've more than paid for your investment.

<Insert Buy Button>

60-Day, "No Wiesel Clause, Money-Back Guarantee!

On top of that, I'm also going to be giving you my 60-day, No-Wiesel clause, money back guarantee.

That means, if you don't think I've delivered on everything I just promised you, I'll give you every single red penny back.

Sound fair?

This is totally **RISK-FREE** and <u>you have nothing to lose</u>.

Thousands of people are already experiencing amazing results because of this system.

They're closing 5 and 6-figure deals on a regular basis.

Imagine if this system got you even 1/10th of the results most people get***... you'd be a CLOSING MACHINE!***

Getting started is simple.

Just click on the button below to get rolling.

<Insert Buy Button>

You could start seeing results as soon as tonight!

<Insert 3 testimonial videos, last video should tell people to take action and buy>

Listen, I could show you videos like this all day long, but without taking action, you'll never know what it's like to be a master closer.

So right now, you have 3 options...

Option #1: You can take everything I just shared with you on this page and say, "thanks but no thanks" and go back to your normal life, with your normal sales and normal bank account.

Option #2: You can take what you learned, dabble a little "here and there" and hopefully see some kind results based on your trial and error.

Or...

Option #3: You can do what most people do and skip past all the hard work. All you have to do is click the button below right now, make a small, one-time investment in your future and start closing more sales, ***faster, while having your customers LOVE you for it – Guaranteed!***

<Insert Buy Button>

Click the button now before something else pops up – I promise, after you order, the only question you'll ask yourself is... *"why didn't I do this sooner"*.

Plus, you're totally covered by my 60 day, money-back guarantee so you literally have nothing to lose!

I guarantee you results <u>or you don't pay!</u>

NO ONE makes offers as crazy as that. I do it because I know that once you order my system, you'll have the ability to start seeing results within hours!

Click the button below right now and let's do this!

<Insert Buy Button>

To Higher Profits And More Sales,

<Insert Blue Color Signature>

Eric Pathi

P.S. Remember, when you order immediately, you'll also get these **3 BIG BONUSES…**

BIG BONUES #1: "Pitch Domination Secrets" – this is where we are role playing pitches, to help you fully understand the content

BIG BONUES #2: "Objection Obliteration Tactics" so you know exactly what to say to diffuse ANY objection and turn it into a sale

And…

BIG BONUES #3: "One-Hitter Quitters" is where we role play simple 1-liners you can start using immediately, this is where most people fall flat on their face

P.P.S. On top of that, you'll also be fully protected by my 60-Day, 100% Money-Back Guarantee.

If you don't like Anatomy Of The Close for ANY reason and don't feel I've delivered on all my promises, simply send me a message asking for a refund and <u>you'll get every single penny back.</u>

I only want your money if you're happy.

<u>Order right now before something else pops up and grabs your attention.</u>

I promise, this will be the best decision you've ever made.

Order now:

<Insert Buy Button>

Turn Your Speakers UP! [add speaker image]

BASED ON REAL EVENTS:
"South America's Hidden Secret To Permanently Eliminating Sickness, Forging Unshakable Self Confidence, Becoming Financially FREE...

...And living a much happier, longer and richer life"

Script starts>>>

It was 3am, all the lights were off in the house.

My friend Julio put his hand over my mouth, woke me up, rushed me out of bed and told me we needed to leave... NOW!

I didn't know what the heck was going on but with the deathly look in my friend's eyes and his head hunched low, I knew I had to keep following him.

We crept down the stairs of his Aunts 2 story home, towards the garage.

She lived in a beautiful plantation style mansion in Cochabamba, Bolivia, surrounded by farm land and mountains.

Once in the garage, Julio whispered to get in the jeep and keep my head down, I did as he said without question.

10 seconds after I laid down in the backseat, Julio quickly sneaked to the door we originally came from to enter the garage...

...and slowly pulled the door shut, but just before he got in the jeep, we heard angry voices speaking in Spanish just outside.

I had no idea what was going on.

Before I could think, Julio hits the garage door open and pulls out a small, rusted, .22 caliber pistol (usually reserved for prostitutes)...

… And we race out of my aunt's home at full speed, crashing into bushes, trash cans and everything else in our way.

Within minutes, 2 other jeeps were behind us, each armed with at least 3 "cocalero's" toting AK-47 rifles and screaming out the window.

Cocalero's are what my friend and I called, cocaine smugglers, dealers, farmers and anyone else in the drug biz.

Julio kept telling me to keep my head down, but with all the swerving and near death crashes, I had to see what the heck was chasing us.

When I realized what was happening, I didn't know what to do!

I was in another country where guns were outlawed and frowned upon… yet these guys chasing us, clearly had no problem getting high powered, fully automatic weapons.

And what was our defense?

My friends .22 caliber pistol he purchased "off the street" – which means, 110% ILLIGAL and UNRELIABLE.

We raced down the mountain side and drove an hour southeast to the small village of Vacas, Cochabamba.

It was there, I met Don Alejandro.

Well, that's what I called him anyway. He told me he was visiting the small village while on his way to explore the Amazon.

After sipping on Coca Tea to help with my altitude sickness from being in the mountains, Don Alejandro explained how he stumbled upon a secret while on his travels which let him "reprogram" his mind.

You see, he told me that years ago, he used to be a very shy person who had a hard time being in public, communicating with others, and what's worse, is he was at a job he hated, where everyone thought he was a "push over."

He was the loaner who everyone picked on in school and shunned from their group.

But once he made a few simple "adjustments" to his thinking, it was like his entire world magically changed… and it happened virtually overnight!

What's truly amazing is, after he made these simple "adjustments" he got offered the job of his dreams and ultimately became a writer who had his own blog and travelled the world, "blogging for profits" as he would often say.

It was then, I realized just how powerful your mind can really be.

It can cause a life of pure misery or a life filled with passion, happiness, and abundance.

My name's **Brian Clark**, and it wasn't just financial riches Don Alejandro was suddenly being blessed with.

See, what he stumbled upon while on this journey was an amazing secret that shows you how to eliminate stress from your life (forever), sky-rocket your self-confidence, wipe away your financial debts and program yourself for unlimited, **lifetime wealth and success.**

And the true beauty is, you can expand your comfort zone, shatter the beliefs limiting your life, and instantly boost your self-esteem forever.

Have you ever wondered, as I have, why some people are successful in life and others live out their lives in fear and failure?

If you've ever wanted to be one of those people who lives out their dreams, then what I'm about to reveal to you in this video, is the most important information you've ever heard in your life.

And here's why...

Did you know there's a single ingredient that separates people who are successful in life from people who are not?

That component is how you use your mind to harness your personal power.

People who use their mind power will take their dreams and make them come true.

They are fearless in their drive and will take immediate, massive, repeated action and will never give up until they can live their dreams.

On the other hand, people who lack this ability still have the same yearnings and desires as everyone else, but they stay stuck and unfulfilled.

They never make their dreams come true.

Their lives are an endless series of "what if" questions they ask themselves.

But until now, success has never been so easy.

You see, many people feel powerless in their lives.

They live forever at the whims of others — you know who I'm talking about...

Those nasty bosses, credit card companies, or others trying to hold them back.

They never discover the secret to incredible power that's already hidden deep within them.

For most people, harnessing this power is just a dream or fantasy.

But, now you can be on the way to achieving your dreams in just minutes.

I know it sounds incredible, but there's a simple, easy to use proven formula which unlocks everything your heart desires, and automatically creates the life you really want.

In fact, everything you ever wanted becomes a reality.

I want you to understand just how close you are to your dreams right now.

Because in just a moment, I'm going to reveal what I discovered through years of researching what Don Alejandro showed me which allows you to harness your inner power and immediately attract everything and anything you desire...

...into your life at the speed of lightning.

Because of this research, I developed my proven Miracle Brain System.

Now, you too can enjoy success in meeting new friends, developing rewarding relationships, finding a better job, becoming financially secure, and create the life you want.

The Miracle Brain System will change your life forever!

You see, the single most important key to living your dreams is by developing your mental power.

No matter what your dream is, you make it a reality when you master this skill.

You'll be able to handle every obstacle along the way.

And you'll be able to move in the direction of your dreams — in just minutes.

You may be stunned when you realize just how high you can climb and how you are being held back by society.

When you're freed from the prison of your fears, your life is entirely new.

And the best part is, it all happens automatically

But, if you procrastinate, you're putting your dreams off — maybe for a few years or maybe forever.

And see, when you delay your dreams, you miss out on life.

The ideal thing, is to live your dreams now, before it's too late.

Just remember, it's important to take some action each and every day, no matter how big or small, as long as it's in pursuit of your dreams.

And the thing is, countless other people just like you who reached their dreams, did so because of using my Miracle Brain System.

You might be watching this video and think you'd like to make some changes in your life.

But sometimes, even though you'd like a better job, to feel closer to your family, or even just feel good about yourself, something inside stops you from taking action.

One of the traits of highly successful and happy people, is they immediately take action.

If you want to make your dreams a reality, like so many before you have done, I want you to focus your attention on what you really desire inside your heart.

Get a picture of what you want.

Make it vivid focused and as real as possible.

You want it to "come alive".

Never before has it been this simple to achieve all your dreams.

And, as you think about your dreams and what's important to you about moving toward your ideal lifestyle, you might realize that we're all either moving toward or away from our dreams at all times.

Maybe part of your dream is to:

- ✓ Get a better job with better working conditions
- ✓ **Or maybe you want to become your own boss**
- ✓ Give yourself weekly pay raises
- ✓ **Secure ANY job regardless of your education, age or skill level**
- ✓ Effortlessly attract anyone you want in your life
- ✓ **Or maybe you just want to become the WINNER you always knew you were**

Because, I'm about to show you how to make your dream come alive, the same way I've done for thousands of my other students who used my course.

Actually, here's some feedback from one of my happy students, Tim Lane...

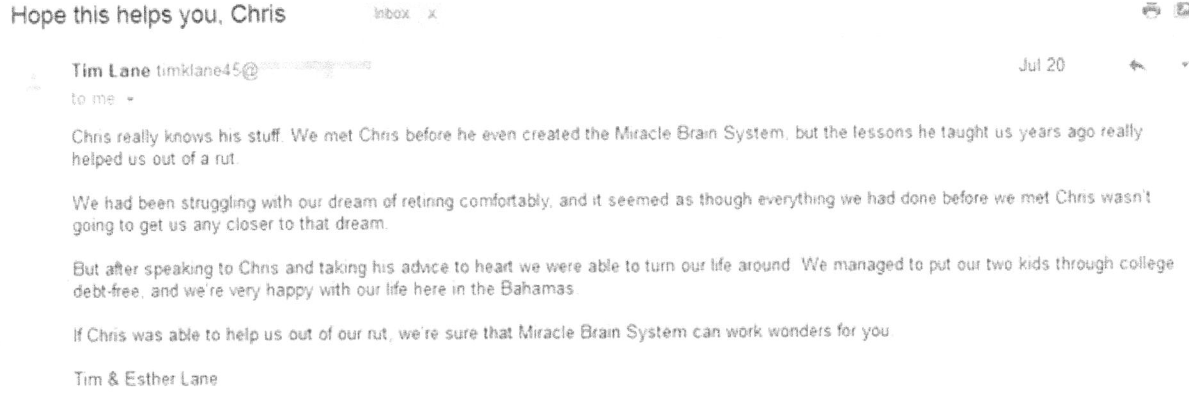

Hope this helps you, Chris Inbox x

Tim Lane timklane45@ Jul 20

to me

Chris really knows his stuff. We met Chris before he even created the Miracle Brain System, but the lessons he taught us years ago really helped us out of a rut.

We had been struggling with our dream of retiring comfortably, and it seemed as though everything we had done before we met Chris wasn't going to get us any closer to that dream.

But after speaking to Chris and taking his advice to heart we were able to turn our life around. We managed to put our two kids through college debt-free, and we're very happy with our life here in the Bahamas.

If Chris was able to help us out of our rut, we're sure that Miracle Brain System can work wonders for you.

Tim & Esther Lane

And then there's Jennifer Green…

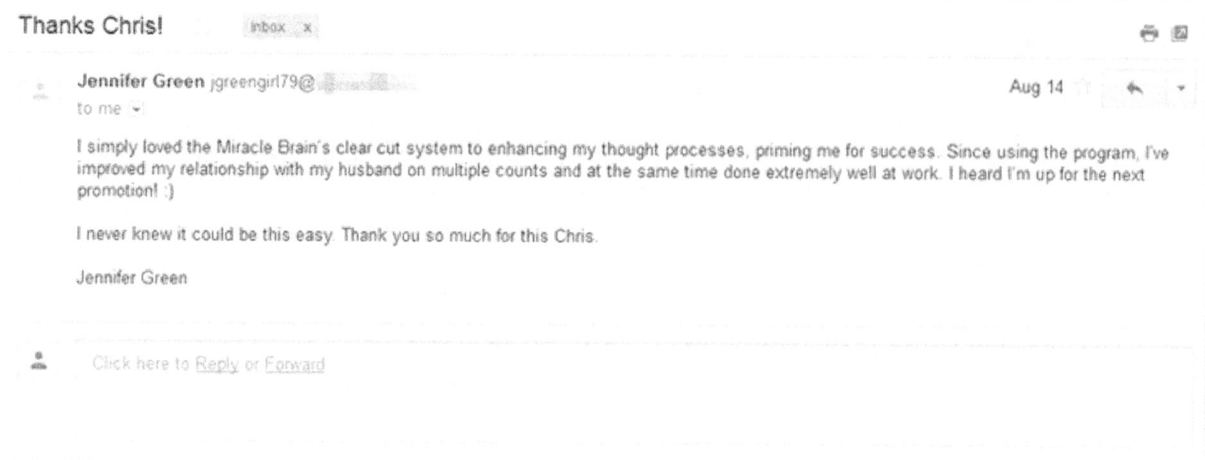
Thanks Chris!

Jennifer Green jgreengirl79@

to me

Aug 14

I simply loved the Miracle Brain's clear cut system to enhancing my thought processes, priming me for success. Since using the program, I've improved my relationship with my husband on multiple counts and at the same time done extremely well at work. I heard I'm up for the next promotion! :)

I never knew it could be this easy. Thank you so much for this Chris.

Jennifer Green

Click here to Reply or Forward

You see, the Miracle Brain System creates wealth, success, romance, helps you lose your unwanted weight and also builds unshakable self-confidence.

You can literally manifest anything you want.

You can even use these methods to find your "true calling" and give your life meaningful purpose and inner peace.

And if you're thinking: "That may have worked for everyone else, but it won't work for me!"

You're dead wrong.

This will absolutely work for you. You'll feel the power winding and unlocking inside you as soon as you dive into your first Mastery lesson.

Unless your personal mind power has already been trained and developed with these techniques, it affects every aspect of your existence.

The way you set your goals, choose your values, or react to life is shaped by who and what we think we are.

When we use our Miracle Brain System power, we have a more confident feeling inside, we become successful in our lives, and we become unstoppable.

What You Discover In This Video Will Change Your Life Forever.

Here's some of what you'll be getting in this system:

- ✓ **How To Develop Your Mind As A Tool Which Can Work Miracles For You And Those Around You** – Discover how a simple man, named Tim made a hair-north of $1,000,000.00 by the time he was 60 using these secrets (and he did it without any risk or hard work)

- ✓ **What You Need To Know To Control You Inner Powers-** Knowing this alone gives you the secret ability actually improve your IQ and overall intelligence – thousands of my students are becoming "geniuses" by using these no-work-needed "conscious mind" techniques

- ✓ **How To Stop Being Ruled By Your Past** – Many times, we fall victim to our past, and using this "simple key" – now makes it possible to move forward effortlessly

- ✓ **How To Use Your Mental Powers Of Intellectual Leverage** – I'll show you an easy way to do much more, with much less "brain power" ... you see, once you're able to use your brain like a computer, you'll be able to get things done faster and better

- ✓ **The Secret Cerebral Power To Overcome "Cloudy" Thinking** – The 3 steps you'll discover in this section will instantly give you the ability to control and banish your unhappy moods

- ✓ **How To Quickly Develop The Forgotten Power Of "Psycho-Photographic Memory"** – Finally, remove the veil over your eyes and gain the awesome ability to register a specific picture in your mind of any memory (no matter how long ago or short it was)... this is the same kind of ability "Super Brains" and geniuses use to gain an unfair advantage over everyone else... think of it like photographic memory on steroids

- ✓ **How To Have Mind-Altering SEX** – Imagine having the ability to have mind-altering sex where you're effortlessly able to take your partner and yourself into exctasy and pure bliss – NO one has ever done this with your partner, and once you get this system, you'll have the power of sexual pleasure at your fingertips – Frankly, because you'll have access to these forgotten cerebral sexual enhancers, you'll have a hard time breaking ties with your partner, they'll be so attached and drawn to you – you'll truly break their heart if you leave them.

Pretty crazy, huh?

But that's not all you'll gain from my course.

I'm dedicated to making this the wisest investment you've ever made in your life.

And listen, the information in this system is worth thousands of dollars. And it's worth every penny isn't it?

Think about it...

... so many people go into debt in order to go to college. Hoping for a high-paying job afterwards.

I've known people who've sank into more than $250,000.00 worth of college tuition debt.

And you know what?

These people end up working at a job they didn't want which makes it almost impossible to pay back that school loan.

And what's worse is they hate their life and come home to bills, television and their choice of either alcohol or drugs just to ease the pain, anxiety and stress.

Wouldn't you agree that it makes more sense to invest $1000 for something you know for a fact will bring you millions of dollars, if you so choose...

While also automatically giving you a happy, long, guilt and stress-free life?

Of course you would.

It's a no-brainer, but to be honest, I'm not going to charge you anywhere near $1000 for this system.

You see, I want to make sure I can get it in as many hands as possible and help as many people as I can.

And to make sure you're guaranteed for success, here's what else you'll be getting in the Miracle Brain System:

- ✓ **The Secret Powers of Profitable Concentration** – You'll understand the 16 secret rules to instantly bringing you more wealth than you ever thought possible

- ✓ **How To Control Your Nervous Tension And Worries** – Never feel that anxious tension run down your neck and spine again, control your emotions, body and life with this lesson on page 111 in the Miracle Brain System handbook

- ✓ **How To Protect Yourself From Being Dominated By Others** – Energy vampires and emotional bullies feed off your energy and pain – you can instantly put a stop to this. The beauty is, you won't even need to confront or talk to these "dominators" – with the simple tips you'll discover in this section of the system, you'll instantly banish these people from your life, or even "turn the tables" on them and make them feel anxious, awkward, scared, and fearful, if you so choose. Honestly, I hope you just dismiss them from your life and move on, but the truth is, you *can* harm them so please be careful

- ✓ **How To Gain Power and Control Over Others** – Imagine being able to talk to your family, coworkers, enemies, and even your mail-delivery person, in a way that makes them do virtually anything you want. It's possible and I urge you to only use the techniques I show you for positive influence

- ✓ **How To Develop PERFECT Judgement** – We've all fallen victim to poor judgment. Sometimes, those bad decisions can affect your relationships, work and your life. Using what I show you on page 159 of the Miracle Brain System handbook, you'll be able to develop PERFECT judgement to make sure you always make the right decisions, especially during tough times

You have abilities and powers you're not even aware of.

And what's amazing is, you were born with these powers — but you never learned how to master them.

Instead you go through life like an unguided missile, trying different things and "hoping for the best" — but never really fulfilling your dreams.

I'll show you how to master these amazing powers and fulfill your dreams with my unique Miracle Brain System.

Doctors and scientists now firmly believe that 75% of all sickness and disease starts in the mind.

Researchers have also proven that stress, which starts in the mind, is the number one cause of all fatigue and illness.

Scientists have also proven that we only use 10% of our mind.

The rest is never used properly.

That means 10% of our mind is causing 75% of all sickness — and we don't even know how to use that 10% properly.

Imagine what would happen if we used our mind to its fullest potential?

We would stop getting sick and start living healthier, more productive lives.

Researchers have also proven that people who have a healthy and positive attitude — or incorporate positive thinking — live better lives.

Why is that?

Because they know how to use the power of their mind.

Unfortunately, most people never get their mind working for them. Instead, they get their mind to work against them — creating things they don't want.

If this is happening to you, I'll show you how to reverse it immediately when you get my system.

You see, this system shows you how to use your mind correctly and it shows you how to instruct your conscious mind so that you create the life you want.

With Miracle Brain System— you'll direct your conscious mind as well as your subconscious mind.

Your mind has unbelievable power. And in this course, I'll show you exactly how to unleash this amazing power.

You'll discover proven techniques which will generate you astounding results.

Throughout your life, you have been taught all kinds of things.

You were taught how to walk, how to read, how to write, etc.

But no one ever taught you how to use the power of your mind.

Miracle Brain System is the instruction book for your mind. You'll begin to attract everything you want in your life as you go through this course.

You have the power — I just show you how to use it. And best of all, the results are guaranteed.

Unfortunately, most people think that in order to change their life or grow as a human being, all they need to do is set goals, plan things ahead, manage their time better, say an affirmation or two, become more disciplined, work with a daily planner and a goal minder.

This is 100% wrong and will only cause you more grief and distance you from your goals.

The gurus who want you to follow such routines are not interested in helping you.

They only want you to continue following them so you become dependent on them and their teachings.

That's the LAST thing I want to do.

There's an old saying: "Give a man a fish and you can feed him for a day. TEACH him to fish and you feed him for life!"

The Miracle Brain System TEACHES YOU TO FISH so you never have to depend on anyone or anything for the rest of your life.

This system makes you unstoppable in business, gives you clarity and vision in your life and lets you live your dreams as you complete your greatest ambitions.

You'll discover the most powerful techniques to quiet your mind and develop your instincts — and intuition — while eliminating stress and enjoying greater fulfillment in every aspect of your life.

You'll accomplish goals you never dreamed possible.

You'll master these powers in my Miracle Brain System — the only complete program that gives you the power to change your life, and is guaranteed to help you accomplish your goals.

Just listen to what Jason Langfield had to say:

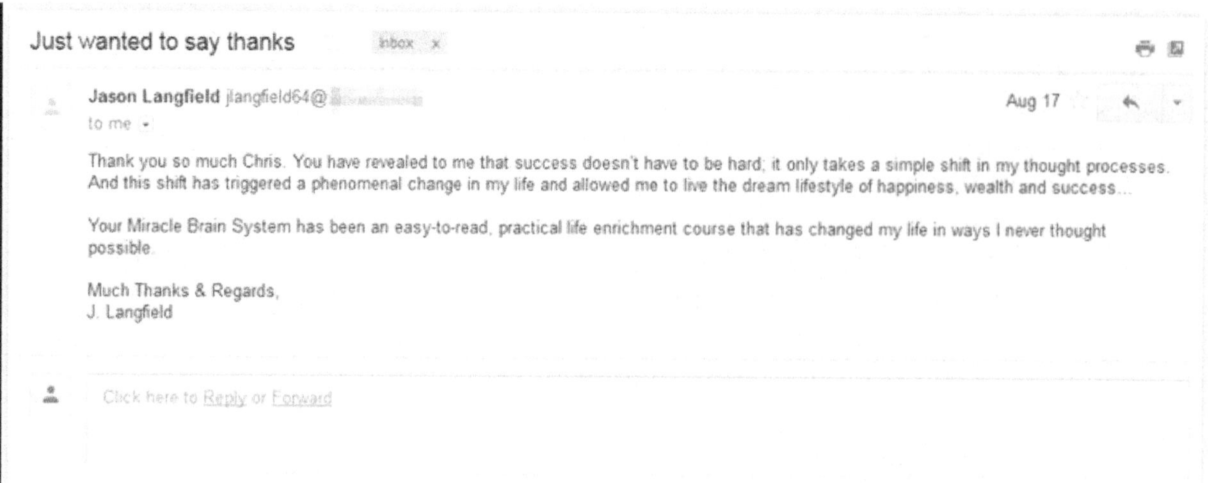
Just wanted to say thanks
Inbox x

Jason Langfield jlangfield64@
to me

Aug 17

Thank you so much Chris. You have revealed to me that success doesn't have to be hard; it only takes a simple shift in my thought processes. And this shift has triggered a phenomenal change in my life and allowed me to live the dream lifestyle of happiness, wealth and success...

Your Miracle Brain System has been an easy-to-read, practical life enrichment course that has changed my life in ways I never thought possible.

Much Thanks & Regards,
J. Langfield

Click here to Reply or Forward

With Miracle Brain System your daily life becomes simple and easy - you'll eliminate stress, worry and anxiety within days or even hours.

You'll also begin creating events you thought would never happen.

With this step-by-step course, you'll understand the principles of the subconscious and discover why short term tapes or subliminal programs don't work.

Miracle Brain System unlocks your ability to do the things you love to do - it shows you how to follow your passion and manifest the life of your dreams.

With Miracle Brain System you follow your dreams - enjoying success after success while increasing your self-confidence with each new day.

And you see, when you have success, you also have passion. When you combine these 2 elements, you fuel your success and destroy obstacles.

And before you have success, you need to have an opportunity.

Right?

With Miracle Brain System you'll create incredible opportunities and know which of those opportunities is best for you.

The confusion and indecision will vanish like a ghost.

When you follow the simple steps outlined, you'll change the way you think – which will get you results for the rest of your life.

Miracle Brain System teaches you how to think so you always send the right messages to your conscious and subconscious mind to create the life you want.

There are hundreds of books, courses, personal coaches, software programs, subliminal tapes and short-term solutions out there that promise to change your life.

But none of them work because they don't teach you HOW to harness your own power already hibernating deep inside you.

Warning!

Your mind plays tricks on you - yes - it deceives you.

It convinces you to stop trying to create change because it might be comfortable where it is4 right now - even if you aren't happy.

Miracle Brain System shows you how to take control of your mind so it starts working for you –immediately!

And you'll quickly discover when your mind is deceiving and playing tricks on you.

And even more importantly, how to reverse its course within minutes.

You see, Miracle Brain System gives you power.

It gives you power over yourself, situations and even those around you.

What you'll be seeing in this system can also be used to harm or even hurt other people, without ever touching them.

Please promise me you won't use these powers for evil.

It would really make me feel terrible if that started happening.

But since I can't control what you do with these techniques, I'll just assume you only have positive intentions.

And listen, the time is NOW to shortcut your way to the life you've always wanted.

It will be like following a clearly laid out road-map.

Here's some more of what you'll be getting in this system:

- ✓ Develop The Power For Always Making The Wisest *Decisions In The Future*
- ✓ Timing Is Everything – Here's How To Make Sure Your "Timing" Is Always PERFECT
- ✓ How To End Your Aching Pains and Illnesses – Forever
- ✓ How To Skyrocket Your Sexual Stamina and Health
- ✓ How To Use Your Natural Hidden Powers To Stay Younger And LIVE LONGER!
- ✓ How To Develop Instant Physio-Magic: The Secret of Perpetual Miracle Mind Magic
- ✓ And there's lots, lots more

Your Future Starts NOW!

[Allow buy button to pop up now]

Okay, So What's The Cost For This Incredible System?

Again, How much would you spend on a personal coach - perhaps a few thousand dollars for a year of work?

And then, add to that price any materials you may have to buy.

Maybe you would spend a few hundred dollars on books, tapes, CDs and other material.

Well, you're not going to pay anything near that.

The amazing Miracle Brain System course usually sells for $249.

But for a limited time if you order by Midnight tonight - Your investment in your future, with the "one of a kind" Miracle Brain System, is only one transaction of just $39.95

And here's my No-Wiesel Clause, 100% 60-Day Money-Back GUARANTEE:

Your success in using the Miracle Brain System is completely guaranteed.

Use the System at MY risk for a full 60-Days.

If at the end of 60 days, you haven't experienced a dramatic change in your life, I want you to ask for a refund.

If at the end of 60 days, you aren't closer to living your dreams, I want you to ask for a refund.

Just shoot me an email, and I'll give you a full return on your money. No questions asked. No hard feelings. No silly "small print" – if you don't see results, you get every single penny back. Period.

Look, you have my permission to use and test this program and if you haven't accomplished your goals, I insist that you return this system and I will quickly refund your money.

You see, you're totally covered here. I've eliminated all the risk and made this as simple as possible.

In fact, on top of my MONEY BACK GUARANTEE, here are **4** more rock-solid GUARANTEES you can count on:

GUARANTEE #1: I guarantee to always deliver the highest quality content in my courses, and this course is no different. You'll be getting the most powerful information available on the internet right now, I truly believe that

GUARANTEE #2: I guarantee to always respond to your questions if you ever send them in. I know what it's like to be stuck, trying to ask for help, and getting no response from the other side – I promise you, when you enroll yourself in this system, my team and I will be with you, every step of the way

GUARANTEE #3: I guarantee you will receive almost instant results while using this system. And what's better is, these results will last forever – imagine yourself becoming happier, healthier, smarter (your IQ score will literally improve), and even more financially secure with that house you always wanted and the car you know you deserve. I promise, with this system, all your dreams can come alive in real life... just give me 60 days, okay? I guarantee your results

GUARANTEE #4: After ordering this system, you'll begin to meet positive new people. This is normal with our students, the universe rewards those who take action on their dreams, and when you order this system, it will reward you. I promise

Plus, when you order by Midnight tonight, you'll also get these incredible additional bonuses valued at more than $200.00 absolutely FREE!

[Insert images for each free gift during each slide for bonuses]

FREE BONUS GIFT #1: The world famous, Think and Grow Rich Audiobook and Manual by Napoleon Hill. Every successful person MUST have this as part of their "success collection"

FREE BONUS GIFT #2: The Law of Success Volumes 1 and 2 by Napoleon Hill. These are the lesser known principles of personal power currently being used by the happiest, richest and healthiest people in the world

FREE BONUS GIFT #3: The Power of Believing, this is a book I wrote showing you how to live life the way you want and on your own terms. I'll be selling it for $97 soon, but you're getting the "pre-release" version, and when you order today – you'll get it FREE

FREE BONUS GIFT #4: Napoleon Hill's "rare" recordings – these are recorded in his own voice and have been used to teach the wealthiest 1% how to easily stay on top for years

Together these **FREE** bonuses are easily worth more than $200 - and they're all yours absolutely **FREE** if you order by Midnight tonight.

Remember - you only get one life - there are no second chances.

Make the most of this life NOW!

It doesn't matter how old you are! It doesn't matter what your situation is.

You can still have everything you want in life when you follow the Miracle Brain System.

Studies of Internet behavior show that if you leave this site and don't try the Miracle Brain System, you will likely never find this site or video again.

And that's really sad because it means, you miss out on your dreams.

People who keep doing the same things over and over again get the same results.

And that will never change.

So come on, order my proven Miracle Brain System techniques - completely and totally risk-free and soon, you'll be singing its praises to others, telling them to get this system also.

The same way our student Sarah Mitchell did:

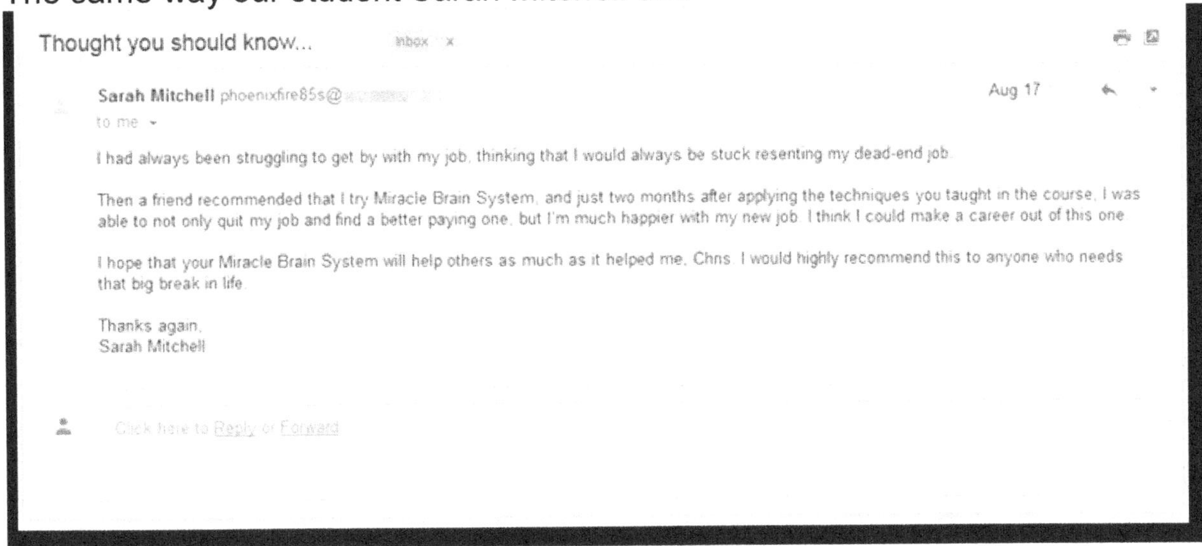
Thought you should know...

Sarah Mitchell phoenixfire85s@

to me

Aug 17

I had always been struggling to get by with my job, thinking that I would always be stuck resenting my dead-end job.

Then a friend recommended that I try Miracle Brain System, and just two months after applying the techniques you taught in the course, I was able to not only quit my job and find a better paying one, but I'm much happier with my new job. I think I could make a career out of this one.

I hope that your Miracle Brain System will help others as much as it helped me, Chris. I would highly recommend this to anyone who needs that big break in life.

Thanks again,
Sarah Mitchell

Click here to Reply or Forward

Get ready to Claim the Life you want.

After you order, circle the date on your calendar.

Why?

Because years in the future, you are going to celebrate this date.

And you'll remember it as the day you stepped up and made a REAL change

I look forward to hearing your transformational story, just like thousands of my other students.

And I hope you send it in also. It would really make my day a lot happier.

So order now!

Frankly, at this moment, you're faced with 3 possible life choices.

And I want you to understand just how serious your decision to these life choices truly is.

What are these choices?

Simple, you have:

CHOICE #1: Which is to leave this page forever and continue on with your life, getting zero results and settling for a life of stress, anxiety, sickness, fear and worst of all, regret for what you WISH you would have done with your life. You'll watch everyone else around you grow and prosper with happy relationships, happy careers and happy families while you stay stagnant and left behind

CHOICE #2: You agree with everything I've spoken about so far and want to make a change, but don't feel like doing anything right now and aren't sure you want to invest in yourself. You can take the information you've discovered and just "hope" to figure it out somehow, someway. Maybe you have success, or maybe you don't. Who knows? If you choose this, good luck, I wish you the best

CHOICE #3: This is the "no-brainer" choice for most people. This is where you click the order button on this page and invest in yourself, your future and your life. This choice is for people who want to be *winners*. This is the choice for people who want change and freedom. ***This really is the only logical solution for you.***

Sometimes we need to take a "leap of faith" in order to become the people we know we can be.

And with my MONEY BACK GUARANTEE – there's absolutely ZERO risk for you to get started. **It's all on me.**

Click on the order button right now, and let's do this together!

[Wait – 15 seconds]

Still haven't ordered?

Look, there's no risk in ordering this program. You have a FULL 60 days to test-drive the techniques.

In fact, if the Miracle Brain System doesn't OUTPERFORM, OUTMOTIVATE, and SUPERCHARGE your life, I want you to return it to me for a full refund. What could be fairer?

Remember, this is the only program on or off the Internet where the author takes personal interest in your success. I know you've failed in the past. I won't let you fail again.

Click the order button below and let's do this!

"Why Am I Getting This?"

Dear <Firstname and Lastname>,

As you can see, this personal letter was sent to you in a "money bag"…

... and once you opened that bag, what came out?

A $1,000,000.000 bill.

Why have I done this?

Actually, there are 2 *very* specific reasons:

REASON #1: I have something very important to share with you and I needed to make sure you opened my "envelope"

And...

REASON #2: Since what I have to share with you can potentially add another 20 to 30 long-term, retainer clients to your list…

… I figured using a *financial "eye-catcher"* seemed especially appropriate.

You see, my name is <insert your name>, and over the last few years my team and I have been working with agencies…

… just like yours who are looking to *automate* their flow of leads and incoming business.

And here's what we've noticed...

…Most agencies are **INCREDIBLE** at serving their clients, getting them results and truly making a *great* relationship with them.

And I'm sure you're probably the same way, right?

I bet your clients probably love working with your agency and they probably can't wait to do more business with you.

Heck, they might even refer business to you!

And that's awesome!

The thing is, even though getting referrals is great, it's simply not *consistent.*

And as you probably know, getting new clients isn't always predictable, either.

Some months you could grab a few great ones…

…And other months, you could be stuck *without any growth* or any *new* (*(Turn page over, please)*

Wouldn't it be amazing if you could literally command *how many* clients you wanted to add to your list each month?

Imagine having the predictability and **<u>control</u>** over how much *extra* money and business you wanted to generate.

It's like having "leads on tap"... *And it works like crazy!*

Nod your head "yes" if you think you'd like to be able to do this in your agency.

"They LAUGHED when I showed this to them, *but when they got the results…"*

I know it might sound a little *weird*, and when I first started showing this to agencies, they laughed at me!

The thing is, those laughs quickly turned into "dropped-jaws" because of how **POWERFUL** and **FAST** this simple system really is.

You see, we've "cracked the code" when it comes to lead generation and we've already successfully applied this to hundreds of agencies just like yours.

And guess what – The results have been OUTSTANDING!

Some of our clients are seeing *small* growths from 2 to 3 new clients per week…
<u>… while others are adding an ***EXTRA*** 20 to 30 per month!</u>

This works almost like magic, it's like printing money on demand!

Listen, I know you might be skeptical.

And who wouldn't?

These results aren't typical, they're EXTRAORINARY!

And we want to show you what we've done to transform these seemingly normal and even "low-level" agencies…

…Into MONSTER powerhouses which can *quickly* generate an influx of new, *quality* clients, while placing them all on long-term, monthly retainers.

Would an extra **2** to **3** new retainer clients per week help your business?

Of course it would!

And that's on the *low end…* using what I'm about to show you will give you almost supernatural abilities when it comes to generating leads.

You'll be known as the "Leads Ninja" by all your peers…
… **you might even get some *HATE* because of how FAST your growth will be.**

But hey, these haters can promote you, while you laugh all the way to the bank. Right?

Go to www.InsertYourLinkHere.com and download your **FREE** Lead Generation Cheat Sheet –

You'll get all the tools you need to start *raking-in* more leads and automate your entire Client Acquisition process.

The best part is, you'll also get our **FREE** video course with the Cheat Sheet so you can start seeing results immediately!

I appreciate you reading this message. **I know you have a super busy schedule and promise to never waste even a second of your time.**

If even 1 thing I said in this letter interests you, make sure you go to our website and grab this Cheat Sheet for yourself.

We're limiting this FREE OFFER to only 21 more people

Here's what to do next…

Go to your computer, type in www.InsertYourLinkHere.com and get instant access to all the "goodies".

After these last 21 people grab it, we're taking the site down.

Why?

Because we're looking to create a few long-term relationships and rather than have millions of people ask to know these tricks, I want to limit it to the people **who want it most.**

Get YOURS and let's kick some butt!

Dedicated To Automating Your Lead-Flow,

(Blue Color Signature)

<Insert your first and last name>

P.S. Make sure you do this before anything else "pops up" and distracts you.

Sometimes in life, we need to take IMMEDIATE action to get the results we want.

And in the process of taking action, other "distractions" will cloud our attention.

Don't get distracted, you are literally one click away from automating your entire lead generation process. This works like gangbusters for other agencies, don't you think there's a chance it could work for you, too?

P.P.S. Listen, let's say you HATE the cheat sheet. The worst thing that will happen is you learned a few cool tactics and then moved on with your life.

But, **what if you experience the same thing hundreds of others already have...** <u>and DRAMATICALLY increase your lead flow, client list and overall BOTTOM-LINE.</u>

Go to www.InsertYourLink.com and get your Cheat Sheet now!

<u>Let's *control your lead flow*, rather than let *it* control you.</u>

COLD CALL SCRIPT

Hey Could I speak with [first name of prospect]?

Great!

Hey, [first name of prospect]...

My name is [Insert your name], have I caught you at a bad time?

ANSWER (yes) or (no) or ("yes but what's this about")

Ok and do you currently doing any online marketing for your company?

ANSWER: (yes) or (no)

Ok great, the whole reason for the call today is actually just to schedule 10 REAL minutes on the phone with you either today or tomorrow, at a better time, to show you how our platform literally does all the marketing and strategizing for you – you pretty much just "set it and forget it."

Does that sound like something you might be interested in?

ANSWER: (yes) or (no)

[IF "NO" – say "thank you" and hang up]

[If "YES"] Ok awesome! And have you heard of our company GotVantage.com?

ANSWER (yes) or (no) – most likely the answer will be a "No"

Oh ok, well what we do is help [insert type of business you're calling, i.e. "plumbing"] businesses just like yours:

- Automate your marketing
- Track your results
- And we also forecast your future sales and recommend specific strategies to boost revenue, based on your results

Does that sound like something you'd be interested in?

ANSWER: (yes) or (no)

[IF "NO" – say "thank you" and hang up]

[If "YES"] Ok awesome! Are you available today? *[if they say "yes" schedule a time, then proceed with script]*

[If "NO"] What time tomorrow works best for you, morning or afternoon?

Ok Great, and does [Insert time] or [Insert Time] work better for you?

Perfect! What's the best email to send you a short Demo video you can check out in the mean time?

Awesome- and what's the best number to send you a reminder text message a few hours before?

Great! Our consultant will call you tomorrow [or today if scheduled] at [Insert scheduled time].

Have a great day, bye!

How To Get Paid To Work In Your Underwear, Even If You've Never Had An "Online Job" Before

You'll discover...

- ✓ **7 Fool-Proof Strategies To Make Companies Chase YOU (No More Applying For Jobs, *HOPING* To Get Picked)**

- ✓ The Simple Secret To Working In Your Underwear (No, This ISN'T Anything Inappropriate)

- ✓ **How To Earn A Full-Time Income Without Going To A Job (This Is EASIER Than You May Think)**

- ✓ And Much, Much More!

Dear Friend,

X years ago, I was struggling to find work and no matter how hard I tried to get a company to hire me... it seemed like I was never the *right fit*.

Frankly, what I really wanted to do was get a company to hire me as a "virtual employee" – that way, I could work on my list of tasks, on my OWN time.

Plus, I wouldn't have to deal with bumper to bumper traffic, annoying co-workers or anything!

The problem was...

I couldn't find a **LEGIT** way to make this happen.

Everything I found online seemed like a total scam, pyramid scheme or complete waste of time.

I'm sure you've run into these sites before, right?

Well, after rummaging through the internet for X days/weeks/months, I was starting to lose hope on ever being able to work from home.

But then, something amazing happened!

I stumbled upon a really simple way to have companies CHASE YOU.

This isn't a "sneaky trick" or any other nonsense, either

It's a foolproof way to start earning a real income... while working from home... in your underwear (if you choose).

Would you like to spend more time with friends and family, working when YOU want... and earning a full-time income?

Imagine the freedom you'll have.

You can wake up when you want, make your own schedule and really OWN your life.

Enter your email in the box below and I'll send you my 7-Steps To Freedom Report, 100% FREE.

No pitching or shenanigans here.

Just real, easy to understand information.

Once you click the submit button, you'll also be taken to another page that has a short # minute video walking you through the exact steps you need to take to get started quickly and start getting paid.

To Working In Your Underwear,

Signature

P.S. Women work harder than men. Period.

And if you'd like to start getting paid a *real* salary, while working from home, the local coffee shop… or *anywhere* you want – you need to enter your email in the box you see on this page.

Just to recap –

I'll send you my 7-Steps To Freedom Report and also take you to a special page that has a short # minute video walking you through the exact steps you need to take to get started quickly, get paid and live life on YOUR terms.

Enter your email now.

100% FREE Video Training

How To Earn $9,500 Per Month Working From Home

(Even if you've never made a dime online before and can barely use a computer)

Dear Friend,

I remember talking to as many people as possible… doing everything I could to bring them into my company.

From cold calling, to cold Facebook messaging.

All the way to SEO, blogging, and TONS of other methods that simply *weren't* cutting it.

It felt like with every encounter, my big smile was getting slapped off my face.

I felt worthless, embarrassed and ashamed… I couldn't get anyone to work with me… let alone listen to what I had to say.

To put it bluntly…

All I wanted to do was crawl up in a corner and die.

In fact, as a network marketer, I was starting to think this kind of rejection was normal.

Heck, everyone said I needed to go through 9 "No's" before getting my 1 "Yes".

Frankly…

<u>That's a bunch of nonsense.</u>

See, this is a *new* world.

A world where more and more people are hitting their 6 and 7 figure goals.

And what's amazing is… they're doing it ***a LOT faster*** than their upline ever did.

As you can imagine… knowing what I'm about to show you on the next page could dramatically change your business, income and even outlook on life…

… but it will also bring envy and jealousy from those "above" you in your organization.

Inside, you'll discover:

- ✓ **How to send simple emails that pay you money (no this is not a chain letter)**
- ✓ How to gain respect, admiration and authority… even if you don't think you deserve it (these secrets are used by celebrities, government officials and high-level entrepreneurs)
- ✓ **How to fire your boss, wake up when you want and still earn more than a doctor, even if you don't have a product or list (yes it's possible and easier than you may think)**
- ✓ How to *effortlessly* influence others using specific psychological triggers (this gives you an almost *unfair* advantage when recruiting new members)
- ✓ **And much, much more**

Enter your email on this page now to get instant access to this **FREE** video training.

I promise, I'll never abuse your email or spam you until you buy my stuff.

This is my way of helping other network marketers, the same way I wanted someone to help me.

Enter your email now to experience the magic of these simple money-making tactics while they're still being shown to you for **FREE**.

Imagine plugging into a system that automatically generated red-hot leads, eager to pay you BIG money to solve their TINY problem...

How To Attract, Sell And Close High-Paying Clients And Earn $100,000 In The Next 90 Days

(This works like magic for consultants, coaches, creatives and agency owners)

VIDEO AUTOPLAYS

Script >>>

I hated waking up every day, desperate to find clients. It's like no matter how hard I tired or how positive I stayed... nothing seemed to really work.

At least not consistently.

You see, X years ago, I was like most consultants.

I'd go through tons of training programs, seminars and read dozens of marketing books published by big-name "experts."

The thing is, a lot of that stuff just didn't fit my style.

I've always been turned off by hard-sell, tricky, gimmicky marketing advice that only tells me how to manipulate people to nail a sale.

You know what I mean?

I wanted to market my programs with integrity, in ways that let me be authentic and feel true to my values.

And if you're a coach, consultant, creative or agency owner, that's exactly what I'm going to show you how to do now.

See in this short video, I'll show you...

- How to make 5 to 6 figures per month (even if you've struggled to make that much in a year)

- How to easily get clients whenever you want (no more *hoping* for clients - we both know, hope is never a good business plan)

- How to have more free time to spend with your family, at a bbq or doing anything you want (while still raking in the cash using simple "plug and play" systems)

My name is Maurice Evans, most folks call me Pastor Moe.

I'm a best-selling author, public speaker and have been featured on CNN, WSJ, USA Today, Entrepreneur Magazine and more.

On top of that, I've also helped hundreds of people go from almost bankruptcy... to consistently hitting 5 and 6-figure months.

That's not to say you'll hit 5 and 6 figure months, there's absolutely no way to guarantee it.

But the tactics I'm about to share with you are reliable and have been proven to work over and over again... like clockwork.

If it's worked for hundreds of other folks, maybe it'll work for you too?

In fact, here's some of the feedback we've been getting from people just like you...

<Insert 3 Testimonials>

We get messages like that every single day, so you can see, this works like crazy, when applied.

When you use what I show you, you could generate $50,000 to $100,000 [Dollars] within the next 90 days.

And that's being conservative.

Heck, even if you're slower at seeing results, it's very possible to still rake in at least $150,000 [Dollars] per year using your current knowledge and experience to make a living.

Imagine having clients pay you $5,000 to $10,000 [Dollars] each for your services while generating a steady stream of 3 to 7 highly qualified leads each week who are eager to speak with you.

If you had a system in place to generate, capture and "pre-sell" those leads on working with you... it wouldn't be very difficult to quickly increase your income.

Would it?

See, charging more and being a highly paid coach, consultant or service provider isn't magic, voodoo or guess work.

It's as simple as putting the *right* message, in front of the *right* people, and giving those people, the *right* method for inquiring about your services.

The thing is, this gets over-complicated way more than it needs to be.

That's why I've created <Name of Product>.

It's my simple, proven system for attracting high-quality leads like clockwork.

And the best part is, I'll show you how to effortlessly close the deal and have your clients thank you for it!

Here's what you're going to get in the <Name of Product>...

<Insert a ton of bullets>

Plus, you'll also get...

<Insert bullets>

This system won't be available forever though.

Frankly, if everyone used it, it wouldn't be as effective.

That's why I'm limiting access to this automated system to only 1000 people.

After that, it'll be locked away in "the vault".

How much is <name of product>

It was originally going to sell for $997 [Dollars]. And frankly, it's worth every penny.

Why?

Because this system is going to help you get high-paying clients who pay you $5,000 to $10,000 [Dollars] each.

Even if you only closed one client, you'd still make back all your money and have a few thousand left over.

This won't cost you $997 [Dollars] though. In fact, it won't even cost you half that.

Right now, while we're still taking new members, you can access the <Name of Product> for only $297 [bucks].

That's a drop in the bucket.

The best part is, it comes with my 100% Money-Back Guarantee!

Life is too short to have bad karma lurking over my shoulder.

That means, if there's any reason you don't think I've delivered on EVERYTHING I said I would, you'll have a full 30 days to get a refund.

No questions, no hard feelings.

If you don't like <name of system>, simply send us an email and we'll refund you every penny.

I know you won't want a refund though.

I'm confident you'll start seeing *predictable* results, just like these folks did...

<Insert 5 testimonials>

Getting started is easy.

Simply click on the link below to order immediately.

I promise, this will be the best decision you ever make.

Plus, it's totally risk-free so you have nothing to lose and literally everything to gain.

Make sure you do this right now though, before anything else pops up on your computer.

This is a digital age, with a lot of digital distractions.

Remember, only the first 1000 people will have access to this system, so if you don't take fast action, you could miss out on this forever.

Right now, there's really only 3 options for you to choose from...

Option #1: You can take everything I just shared with you on this page and say, "thanks but no thanks" and go back to your normal life, with your normal sales and normal bank account.

Option #2: You can take what you learned, dabble a little "here and there" and hopefully see some kind results, based on your trial and error.

Or

Option #3: This is the most popular option. You can skip past all the hard work, leap-frog to the front of the line and apply the secrets shown to you in <name of product> to start earning more money, right away!

I would choose option 3 if I were you... it's RISK-FREE and you literally have NOTHING to lose.

So click the button below right now to get started immediately!

-
-
-
-
-

If they are still there after 5 seconds...say this...

Are you still there?

You probably haven't ordered yet for a few very practical reasons.

In fact, let me address some of those reasons now just to put your mind at ease...

<Insert 10 FAQs>

Now before anything else pops up and distracts you, click the button below immediately to secure your order of <insert name of product>

Remember, we're limiting this to the first 1000 fast-movers and with thousands of people already viewing this same video right now, you need to act fast before missing out on this offer forever!

Click below to get started now!

If you are a small to mid-size business, you NEED to read every word of this letter…

"AMAZING New 'Pad-Lock' Effortlessly Eliminates 'Hack Attacks', Viruses And ALL Internet Issues In Your Business"

…The BEST part is, It's So EASY and SIMPLE to set up, even a 5th grader could do it!

Dear Friend,

You're reading this letter because you're on my preferred "VIP" list and because you've invested in the products we provide at our company.

And here's the deal: The *current* router (or *routers)* you are using in your business are out of date…

… And could be a liability to your company's security, internet speed and *overall performance.*

Actually, are you having internet issues such as:

- Your web pages freezing up
- **Waiting forever for your browsers to load**
- Or maybe you've suddenly started experiencing issues with *other* applications within your computer…

…if you're currently experiencing **ANY** of these "symptoms," you'll want to pay *very* close attention to what I'm about to say *next.*

You see, I've cracked the code on these issues, but before I let you in on this, *we need to make sure this is even something you would want.*

And that's why, if you say "YES" to any one of these 4 questions, you'll want to read every word of this letter…

QUESTION 1: Does your business rely on having *fast* and reliable internet connection?

QUESTION 2: Do you want your customers, clients or patients, who are walking into your business, to have a separate, secure and dedicated "Guest WIFI" login *(this lets you offer WIFI to your customers while not slowing down or affecting your business' connection)*?

QUESTION 3: Do you want to put a "pad lock" on your connection and "lock-down" your business from hackers or potential threats?

QUESTION 4: Do you want to expand your wireless range to have fast internet connection, anywhere inside or outside of your office?

Did you nod your head "YES" to at least one (or more) of these questions?

If so, ***then I guarantee,*** *this will be the most important letter you've ever read, and here's why:*

You see, I'm making you a **"CERTIFIABLY AWESOME"** offer that will expand the physical coverage of your internet, lower your costs, BOOST your internet speed…

…**AND, make accessing your businesses files, WIFI, and overall connection,** ***harder to break into than Fort Knox!***

This makes it virtually **IMPOSSIBLE** for hackers and other threats to *creep* inside your system and steal, delete or totally destroy your entire network.

Does that peek your interest?

If it does, then you will love the WiNG Express!

(WiNG Express Photo)

As a matter of fact, the #1 reasons people love WiNG Express is because it's extremely user-friendly and easy to use.

"It's so easy, a 5th grader can do it"

Listen, I understand that you're not a "guru" in setting all of these "tech" things up, and that's why we pride ourselves on how simple everything is to get started.

It's also why WiNG Express also offers a simple management system which you can access at a single access point – **making your network *really* easy to manage and control with just one router (while still running faster than any *older* models).**

You see, these *older* models I'm talking about require your office to have multiple routers to make your internet **faster simply because they get *too* "overloaded" *with too many* wireless connections, like:**

- Cell Phones

- **Laptops**

- Tablets

- **Even certain camera's and camcorders can connect to your WIFI**

And remember, with WiNG Express, you'll have FASTER internet than what you're currently used to, anywhere in your office (no more "lost signals").

"But… What If I Want SUPER, *Lightning Fast* Connection?"

The true beauty is, if you *do want to* set up multiple access points and get *10X more speed*, these points will discover each other automatically and connect accordingly…

…allowing your network to be fully functional – without you having to setup each access point individually.

This automates everything for you – all you'll need to do is "set it and forget it"…

…the WiNG Express works almost like magic and connects itself with all the access points.

If you are a small to mid-size business, *you need to know something…*

In order to **scale up**, avoid the *new* internet risks coming out every day, and grow your client-base, you NEED to get this for your business…

… and if you still have questions or would like to place your order…

…Call ###-###-#### right now!

One of our "Happy Client Support" staff members will answer every one of your questions and get you started immediately.

And, to make this decision even easier for you, you can also trade in you "old gear" to get a STEEP discount on the WiNG Express – you'll get our special CASH-back "hookup."

That way, you're "out with the old" and "in with the new" – and you get CASH back at the same time for your trade in.

Sounds pretty awesome, right?

Listen, thank you for investing in our products in the past, it means a lot knowing you trust us enough to advise you on the best and most effective solutions for your company.

And that's why I know you'll love the WiNG Express.

Call us now, before you forget about this letter and something else "pops up" – the number again is, XXX-XXX-XXXX

Just tell whoever answers the phone that you got this letter and ***that you're a VIP member***, and we'll take care of the rest.

Thank you so much for reading and I appreciate your business.

To Better "Connections,"

Signature [In blue color ink]

P.S. Remember, if you're even slightly interested in saving money, getting FASTER internet, having an *extremely* secure network…

… and doing it without *ANY* hassles, then call right now at **XXX-XXX-XXXX**

I promise to make this the *wisest* decision you've ever made.

Here's a recap of some of the benefits you'll be getting when you grab WiNG Express, right now:

- **Much faster internet speed** – you won't need to worry about internet "drops" or any other sudden "crashes" ruining your day and screwing up what you need to get done, simply because the "internet is too slow"

- **Higher Level Security** – New viruses, cracks and hacks are being created every day to infiltrate your system and steal your information as well as your customers information… and as you know, the last thing you want, is the liability of having your customers information EXPOSED, because your security *wasn't* "tight enough"

- **Guest Access Set Up** – If you've ever been asked "do you guys have WIFI?" and wanted to say yes, then you will love being able to service your customers with FREE WIFI, while also NOT clogging up your own servers because you're "overloading" it – this makes it a *cinch* to have greater internet speed without your "guests" slowing you down or compromising your companies security

Here's the number again: XXX-XXX-XXXX

Thank you for your purchase! Your payment went through...

1 - Checkout > 2 - Customize Order > 3 - Instant Access

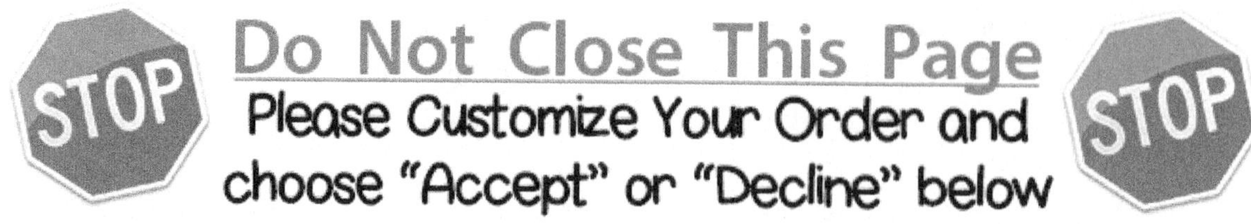

STOP
Do Not Close This Page
Please Customize Your Order and choose "Accept" or "Decline" below
STOP

Do NOT hit the "Back" button. This will cause errors in your order.

Watch This Short # Minute Video For Your Special One Time Upgrade Opportunity:

Autoplay Video

<Make Buy Button and Guarantee Copy Pop Up At The Close of The Video, this is a timed-delay>

Script/Copy:

Hey,

Vas here again...

Real quick, make sure you stay on this page and don't hit the back button because it could cause errors in your order.

I want to congratulate you for investing in WP Speedy PRO.

I guarantee, this is the best investment you've ever made and I can't wait for you to start seeing all the amazing results, the same way hundreds of other folks before you have because of this plugin.

You'll be able to …

- ✓ Quickly speed up your website to lighting speeds
- ✓ Increase your search engine rankings
- ✓ Drive more sales
- ✓ And much, much more

Because you've taken fast action, I want to make you a special one-time offer. That means, if you don't take advantage of it now… you'll miss out on it forever.

Here's my special offer to you…

Thousands of business owners are losing money because of their site's loading time is dangerously slow.

And these business owners need someone to help them out.
And that someone could be you.

They're willing to pay anywhere between $500 for a simple upgrade **or even a few thousand.**

All YOU have to do, is install WP Speedy PRO onto their site and it'll do all the work for you.

Your clients will think you're a total Tech God and if you're smart, you'll have them put you on a monthly retainer to help them with all their websites.

You Can Build A Real, Sustainable Business With Predictable Monthly Cash Flow - Effortlessly

You can charge anywhere between $1500 per month… all the way to $2500 per month.

Imagine having even 3 of those retainer clients paying you monthly.

That's enough for some folks to quit their day job and do this full time.

The thing is, you can get those kind of results, doing this as a part time "hustle".

So, for today only, you can invest in a special license that lets you use WP Speedy PRO on as many sites as you want.

It's unlimited!

SPECIAL BONUS!

And, as an extra bonus, you'll also have the resell rights to WP Speedy PRO, which means you can package it up and resell the plugin yourself, if you choose.

This is a simple way to build a steady 7 or $8,000.00 per month income, part time. How much is this upgrade?

Originally, it was going to sell for $297... and why not, it's worth every penny. *But right now...*

It's only $67 per year or $97 every 3 years.

Most smart marketers just upgrade to the $97 package because you can make back your money within 24 hours if you wanted.

On top of that, if there's any reason you're unhappy, you're still 100% covered by my...

30 Day, No Wiesel Clause, Money Back Guarantee

That means, if you don't feel like you made the right decision, you can still get all your money back.

This is a completely **RISK-FREE** offer that's a no-brainer to take advantage of. Choose which option works best for you and upgrade now by clicking the button below.

<make this section below look like a coupon with a checkbox they can click, insert 30 day guaranteed symbol / should also be included at the top under the VSL with a timed-delay>

Yes! Please add this incredibly generous offer for an unlimited site license with **BONUS** resell rights as a special upgrade to my order right now for only $67 per year or $97 for 3 years.

I understand that I am 100% covered by WP Speedy PRO's 30 Day Money Back Guarantee, so if I am ever unhappy for ANY reason, I am safe and can still get ALL my money back... making this totally **RISK-FREE**

<$67 button>
<$97 button>

Warning: **This is the only time you will ever see this offer.**

Once you leave this page, this offer will be gone forever.

This exclusive offer is only available for customers who just purchased today.

If you're not interested in this one time deal and you want to pass up on this money-making opportunity, just click the "Decline" link at the bottom of the page...

Decline - No thank you, I rather struggle and lose money than quickly speed all my websites up to lighting speed. <make a link>

Wrapping Up

The ability to sell from your words and make huge profits is an art. Thankfully, it is also a skill that can be learned and honed.

After fully understanding the principles taught in this book, you'll have the power to sell almost anything, to anyone...even if you "suck" at selling face-to-face.

You can make potential customers WANT to buy your sh*t. It's amazing.

When writing direct response copy, remember that your job is generally to persuade and influence action.

Some times that takes pissing your reader off, and sometimes that means knowing how to really relate to your reader on a *deeper* level.

Your job as a marketer is to diligently practice these methods on a daily basis.

The more copy you write, the better you will get and soon, you'll be able to churn out high quality sales copy *with ease.*

Don't be discouraged if your sales copy ***doesn't*** convert well the first time.

We've all been there.

The thing is, you don't want to get too discouraged.

Learning to lose is just as important as learning to win.

In fact, it makes you appreciate "being on top" because you'll know what it's like when things weren't always so good.

Keep tweaking your copy, remove the things that don't work and replace them with things that *do.*

Split testing is the key to mastering the art of copywriting.

The better you get, the *faster* you get too.

As the great Bruce Lee said…

"Absorb what is useful, reject what is useless and add what is specifically your own."

#KeepCrushingIt

<u>Keep In Contact</u>

Facebook.com/CarlosRedlich

Facebook.com/carlos.redlich.3
(personal account)

Made in the USA
Monee, IL
29 November 2019